LOHFELD
CONSULTING
GROUP, INC.

10 steps to creating high-scoring proposals

A modern perspective on proposal development
and what really matters

By Bob Lohfeld

Edited by Beth Wingate

**LOHFELD
CONSULTING
GROUP, INC.**

10 steps to creating high-scoring proposals

A modern perspective on proposal development and what really matters

By Bob Lohfeld
Edited by Beth Wingate

Published by Lohfeld Consulting Group, Inc.
940 South River Landing Road
Edgewater, Maryland 21037

For more information, contact BWingate@LohfeldConsulting.com
Production, Design, and Copyediting: Alexandra Wingate and Beth Wingate

|Dedication

We dedicate this book to our outstanding team of capture and proposal consultants who spend their days (and sometimes nights and weekends!) helping our customers to create high-scoring proposals and to our leadership team without whom none of this could happen.

We extend our continuing thanks to our colleagues for your positive reviews of our books and continuing encouragement in sharing our insights and tips with our capture and proposal community.

|About the author & editor

| Author

Bob Lohfeld, Chairman of the Board & Founder, APMP Fellow

Bob Lohfeld has more than 30 years' experience winning contracts in the government market and is recognized consistently for his leadership in business development, capture management, and winning proposals development.

In 2003, he founded Lohfeld Consulting Group to provide capture and proposal services to companies doing business with government organizations worldwide. Today, Lohfeld Consulting Group is one of the leading companies in this market having helped over 350 companies write winning proposals and win billions in new contracts.

Bob teaches Capture Management, and he writes the Capture Management column in *Washington Technology*. In 2012, he was inducted as a Fellow in the Association of Proposal Management Professionals (APMP).

Prior to forming Lohfeld Consulting Group, Bob served as Division President at Lockheed Martin, Vice President of Lockheed Martin Information Technology, Senior Vice

10 steps to creating high-scoring proposals
A modern perspective on proposal development and what really matters

President at OAO Corp., Systems Engineering Manager at Computer Sciences Corp. (CSC), and Program Manager at Fairchild Industries. He also taught at the graduate level at George Washington University School of Engineering Administration.

Bob has served on the Board of Directors for APMP and its National Capital Area Chapter (APMP-NCA) and as Chairman of the American Council on Technology Industry Advisory Council (ACT/IAC), Vice Chairman of the Technology Council of Maryland (TCM), and Board Member of the Armed Forces Communications and Electronics Association (AFCEA), Government Electronics and Information Association (GEIA), and Juvenile Diabetes Research Foundation (JDRF Capital Region). He is a three-time winner of *Federal Computer Week's* Federal 100.

| Editor

Beth Wingate, President, APMP Fellow

Beth Wingate has more than 25 years' proposal development, management, training, and communications/social media experience. She helps clients develop proposals, improve their proposal operations, and train their teams in proposal management best practices. Beth has spent her career finding ways to use technology to enhance teams' business processes and customer deliverables. She specializes in managing responses to large federal government procurements as well as task order proposals.

Prior to joining Lohfeld Consulting, she served as proposal center director for Lockheed Martin and before that for 12 years as proposal center director for Management Systems Designers, Inc. (MSD) (acquired by Lockheed Martin).

Beth was inducted as an APMP Fellow in 2010. She is APMP's 2014 Past CEO, 2013 CEO, 2012 COO, 2010–2011 Director of Education, and 2008 and 2009 President of the APMP-NCA Chapter. She served as the Chapter's *Executive Summary* Newsletter Chairperson, publisher, and editor from 2005 to 2007.

In 2008, Beth received the Steven S. Myers Award for APMP Chapter Chair of the Year. She regularly presents at APMP International and Regional conferences and writes for APMP publications. She has been an active APMP member since 1996.

10 steps to creating high-scoring proposals

A modern perspective on proposal development and what really matters

Contents

10 steps to creating high-scoring proposals
A modern perspective on proposal development and what really matters

10 steps to creating high-scoring proposals
A modern perspective on proposal development and what really matters

10 steps to creating high-scoring proposals

A modern perspective on proposal development and what really matters

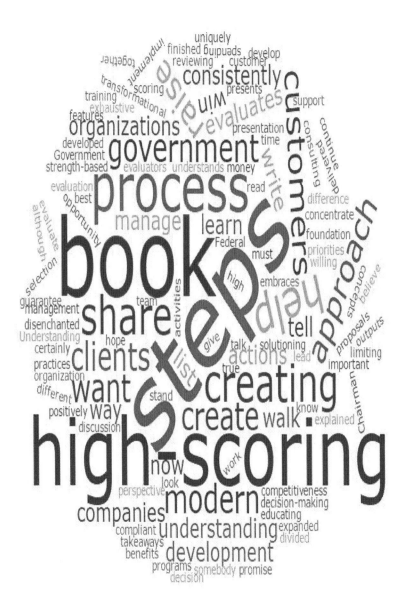

Introduction

Introduction

Beth Wingate, President

Bob Lohfeld developed the *10 steps to creating high-scoring proposals* presentation that he and I expanded into this book to share our *modern perspective* on proposal management and what matters within the proposal process with our customers.

We're using these 10 steps to help our customers concentrate on what's really important in proposal development and on best practices that may have fallen to the wayside because of different priorities within their organizations.

In this book, Bob will walk you through the source selection decision-making process and what the government evaluators and the final decision maker look for as they review your proposals.

He'll cover our strength-based solutioning process and the difference between features and benefits—and how to really make your proposal stand out.

Finally, Bob will walk you through 10 actions your organization can take that will positively affect your proposal outputs.

10 steps to creating high-scoring proposals
A modern perspective on proposal development and what really matters

The concepts and actions Bob presents have been transformational for quite a few organizations. We hope the same will be true for yours.

Bob Lohfeld, Chairman of the Board

When companies engage us to develop their proposal process, to manage their proposal activities, and to write proposals for them, they expect us to do more than just come in and create a proposal that's finished on time and is delivered to the customer. (We work on about 400 proposals each year.)

What we promise them—and what they expect from us—is that we'll come in and help them create a *high-scoring* proposal, and they will continue to use us if they win. If we merely help them to submit compliant proposals and they don't win, then those companies will soon become disenchanted with spending money on an outside proposal team to come in and help support them.

Because we must drive proposals to be high scoring, we put together this presentation—and now this book. We've been educating our customers about our modern approach to proposals, and they come back to our consulting practice and say, "We want you to give us somebody who understands and embraces this approach and will lead us in a way to create high-scoring proposals."

10 steps to creating high-scoring proposals
A modern perspective on proposal development and what really matters

What I want to do now is share with you what I tell the clients when I have an opportunity to talk with them.

We've divided this book into two parts. Part 1 is a bit of a tutorial about how the Federal Government evaluates proposals—what happens to your proposal when it leaves your office. As I tell our clients, don't zone out while I share this tutorial piece because I guarantee you will learn things in it that you didn't know before.

Understanding how the government evaluates your proposals and reviewing our list of takeaways from the evaluation process lays the foundation for understanding Part 2 of the book. I share 10 steps from our modern approach to proposal development that I believe are uniquely us and that raise the competitiveness of our clients' proposals and result consistently in high-scoring proposals.

We limited the book to cover just 10 steps for creating high-scoring proposals, although there are certainly more steps a company can take to raise its proposal score. By limiting the book to 10 steps, we hoped it would be short enough that it could be read easily on a 2-hour airplane flight versus an exhaustive list of steps that not many people would be willing to plow through.

In practice, there are more than 10 steps we take to raise proposal scores, but that is a discussion for another day. If you devote the next 2 hours to understanding how the government is going to evaluate your proposal and how you'll implement the 10 steps explained in this book, then you will be well on your way to consistently creating high-scoring proposals.

If you want to learn more about creating high-scoring proposals, then please visit our website at www.LohfeldConsulting.com where you can retain us to manage and write your proposals or enroll in one of our many training programs.

10 steps to creating high-scoring proposals
A modern perspective on proposal development and what really matters

10 steps to creating high-scoring proposals
A modern perspective on proposal development and what really matters

Part 1 – How the Federal Government evaluates proposals

Objectives of a high-scoring proposal

 Create a proposal that outscores your competition and has no weaknesses, deficiencies, or risks

As a former large company executive, I would bring the proposal team together and say, "Here's what I want you to do. I want you to create a proposal that outscores our competition, has no weaknesses, no deficiencies, and no risks and if you do that and we price it right then we'll win." And giving that clear instruction to everybody, I'd depart and leave them to it.

Well, it's great to make this proclamation, but it's not too practical from the point of view of execution unless you really understand how the government evaluates proposals—what the government does to separate one bidder from the others.

If we're not going to have any weaknesses, deficiencies, or risks in our proposal, we need to understand what constitutes a weakness, a deficiency, and this thing called *risk*.

10 steps to creating high-scoring proposals
A modern perspective on proposal development and what really matters

And then because most of the work that we do is done in best value tradeoff procurements, we really need to understand how price gets traded off against all these non-cost factors.

I want to jump into that and explore with you how the government evaluates proposals.

How the government evaluates proposals

 Proposal evaluation is an assessment of the proposal and the offeror's ability to perform the _prospective_ contract successfully. FAR 15.305

If you go to the Federal Acquisition Regulations (FAR), it tells you explicitly how the government is going to evaluate proposals. For a document written by lawyers for procurement professionals, the first thing I was amazed at is that the instructions for evaluating proposals are only four sentences long. Yet, these four sentences are profoundly insightful to us in how the government will evaluate proposals. I'm going to talk about each of the four sentences and give some background to you on them and how they're interpreted and how they're used in the evaluation process.

FAR Part 15.305 Proposal Evaluation (4 sentences)

1. Proposal evaluation is an assessment of the proposal and the offeror's ability to perform the _prospective_ contract successfully.

2. An agency _shall_ evaluate competitive proposals and then assess their relative qualities solely on the _factors and subfactors_ specified in the solicitation.

3. Evaluations may be conducted using *any rating method or combination of methods*, including color or adjectival ratings, numerical weights, and ordinal rankings.

4. The relative *strengths, deficiencies, significant weaknesses, and risks* supporting proposal evaluation shall be documented in the contract file.

I want to address the first sentence, **"Proposal evaluation is an assessment of the proposal and the offeror's ability to perform the <u>prospective</u> contract successfully."** I've underlined the word *prospective* because a proposal is not a history lesson. It's not a project report on what the company has done for the past 5 years. A proposal begins at the point where the company says, "If you select us, this is what we're going to do for you for the next 5 years or 10 or whatever the period of performance is." It is all prospective.

Now history and past performance are important, but the proposal is not a history lesson, and it's not a report card on your past 5 years with the client. It's always forward looking.

We often find companies write history reports as incumbent contractors and then are stunned that they don't win. So, *prospective* is the first key term in this.

Factors and subfactors are key

 An agency shall evaluate competitive proposals and then assess their relative qualities <u>solely on the factors and subfactors</u> specified in the solicitation. FAR 15.305

The second sentence in FAR 15.305 says, **"An agency shall evaluate competitive proposals and then assess their relative qualities <u>solely on the factors and subfactors</u> specified in the solicitation."**

In government-speak, the word *shall* means it's mandatory. You *shall* and you *shall not* do anything other than what you shall do here. You'll evaluate and assess relative qualities solely—exclusively—on factors and subfactors. So, the Federal Government's evaluations are strictly around the factors and subfactors listed in the solicitation.

Now this came about in the history of the FAR, when early in my career there was a procurement evaluated in the Navy. The evaluation team presented their findings to the admiral, and the admiral basically told the evaluation team, "I want Company ABC to get the contract because I went to the Naval Academy with the president of that company. I trust him with my life and I know he'll do a great job for our Navy."

10 steps to creating high-scoring proposals
A modern perspective on proposal development and what really matters

The award went to the company of his classmate as the admiral directed. A competitor filed a protest, and the protest results came back with GAO ruling that the government cannot have a hidden evaluation criteria. You can't have a stealthy criterion that's not disclosed to all bidders. You must evaluate **solely** on the evaluation factors and subfactors, and if being a Naval Academy graduate was to be an evaluation factor, you must so disclose it in the RFP. Well the award was overturned. The admiral went on to obscurity, but laid a solid foundation in the FAR for what constitutes an acceptable evaluation.

This definition stood for many years, up until about 6 years ago when the government decided—and the GAO decided—that this was too rigorous an implementation for the government, and they broadened it out with what we call the *Nexus Argument*.

This came from a protest launched by Raytheon in July 2011. GAO came back with their finding and said, "Agencies may properly <u>apply evaluation considerations that are not expressly outlined in the solicitation</u> if those considerations are reasonably and logically encompassed within the stated evaluation criteria, i.e., there must be a clear nexus between the stated and unstated criteria."

Well, lo and behold the government opened this up to say that you can use evaluation criteria that aren't expressly identified in the solicitation as long as they're logically encompassed within the stated evaluation criteria. In effect, GAO reversed their decision to some extent.

In practice, what this has done is open up evaluations so if you have features in your offer that can help the agency accomplish its mission, then those features can be considered in the evaluation. If they're meritorious, you can be given credit for them in comparing one proposal against another.

Think about the Federal Aviation Administration (FAA). You might be preparing your proposal for a communications systems procurement, but if there's some feature in your offer that improves air traffic safety, that feature will be meritorious to the agency. It will be reasonably and logically encompassed within the stated evaluation criteria, and you can get credit for it. This is the Nexus Argument or the *mission argument* that broadens out the very narrow definition that was laid down previously.

Rating methods are important...strengths are critical

Evaluations may be conducted using any rating method or combination of methods, including color scores or adjectival ratings, numerical weights, and ordinal rankings. FAR 15.305

Let's examine the third sentence.

"Evaluations may be conducted using any rating method or combination of methods, including color scores (which we all know well—the blues, greens, yellows, and reds) **or adjectival ratings** (it's an *excellent* proposal, a *very good* management plan, a *good* technical section), **numerical weights** (which we see in NASA procurements—the company got 840 points out of 1,000 scale), **and ordinal rankings.**

I've never seen an ordinal ranking used, and I doubt that it ever will be, but the color, adjectival, and occasional numerical weights are pretty common in our procurement process.

10 steps to creating high-scoring proposals
A modern perspective on proposal development and what really matters

Adjectival rating	Definitions NASA Source Selection Guide	Percentile range
Excellent	A comprehensive and thorough proposal of exceptional merit with one or more significant strengths. No deficiency or significant weakness exists.	91–100
Very Good	A proposal having no deficiency and which demonstrates over-all competence. One or more significant strengths have been found, and strengths outbalance any weaknesses that exist.	71–90
Good	A proposal having no deficiency and which shows a reasonably sound response. There may be strengths or weaknesses, or both. As a whole, weaknesses not off-set by strengths do not significantly detract from the offeror's response.	51–70
Fair	A proposal having no deficiency and which has one or more weaknesses. Weaknesses outbalance any strengths.	31–50
Poor	A proposal that has one or more deficiencies or significant weaknesses that demonstrate a lack of overall competence or would require a major proposal revision to correct.	0–30

Figure 1. NASA Source Selection Guide.

10 steps to creating high-scoring proposals
A modern perspective on proposal development and what really matters

Using the adjectival ratings from the NASA Source Selection Guide in *Figure 1* above, if you wanted to score a company as having an *excellent* proposal, what would constitute an *excellent* proposal?

The NASA Source Selection Guide defines an *excellent* proposal as "A comprehensive and thorough proposal of exceptional merit with one or more significant strengths. No deficiency or significant weakness exists."

If your proposal at the factor or subfactor level meets this criterion, then you can get an *excellent* score for that factor. To be *excellent*, your management plan must have one or more significant strengths. In NASA, they take this adjectival rating of *excellent* and break it out numerically. For example, you can receive an *excellent* rating and get 91 points out of 100 or receive *excellent* and get 97 points out of 100. They have a little finer evaluation scale, but the foundation rests on having one or more significant strengths.

A *very good* proposal as they write it here is "A proposal having no deficiency and which demonstrates over-all competence. One or more significant strengths have been found, and strengths outbalance any weaknesses that exist." You can see in *Figure 1* how they define *good, fair,* and *poor*.

DoD color and adjectival rating method

The U.S. Department of Defense (DoD) takes a little different approach. This new Source Selection Procedure was just published at the end of March 2016. It's an update of the one that was published 5 years earlier.

They use five color scores and that's a nice thing because we have a very symmetrical evaluation with the five color scores. Blue is best, purple is next best, green means it's okay—it's acceptable—yellow is marginal, and red means you really wish you hadn't bid.

They also use a slightly different adjectival score of *outstanding, good, acceptable, marginal*, and *unacceptable*.

The DoD Source Selection Procedure defines what constitutes an outstanding evaluation score or a blue score, and it reads as follows, "Proposal indicates an exceptional approach and understanding of the requirements and contains <u>multiple strengths</u>."

10 steps to creating high-scoring proposals
A modern perspective on proposal development and what really matters

Color	Adjectival rating	Definitions DoD Source Selection Procedure
Blue	Outstanding	Proposal indicates an exceptional approach and understanding of the requirements and contains <u>multiple strengths</u>.
Purple	Good	Proposal indicates a thorough approach and understanding of the requirements and contains <u>at least one strength</u>.
Green	Acceptable	Proposal indicates an adequate approach and understanding of the requirements.
Yellow	Marginal	Proposal has not demonstrated an adequate approach and understanding of the requirements.
Red	Unacceptable	Proposal does not meet requirements of the solicitation and, thus, contains one or more deficiencies and is unawardable.

Figure 2. DoD Source Selection Procedure.

Wow! Multiple strengths! To be *good*—a purple—you must have a "thorough approach and understanding of the requirements and contain[s] <u>at least one strength</u>."

So, multiple strengths make you blue and one strength makes you purple. A green proposal is adequate and there's nothing particularly noteworthy about it, and then yellow, which is marginal, and so on down the scale.

10 steps to creating high-scoring proposals
A modern perspective on proposal development and what really matters

The foundational definition in both NASA and DoD is based on **strengths**, so if you strive to have a high-scoring proposal, your proposal must be rich in features that can be scored as strengths. If there are no strengths, the best score your proposal can get is a mediocre grade.

Typical evaluation terminology

The relative strengths, deficiencies, significant weaknesses, and risks supporting proposal evaluation shall be documented in the contract file. FAR 15.305

The fourth sentence—the final sentence in the FAR instruction about evaluating proposals—just knocked me over when I read it the first time.

It says, **"The relative <u>strengths, deficiencies, significant weaknesses, and risks</u> supporting proposal evaluation shall be documented in the contract file."**

Wow! The strengths, deficiencies, and weaknesses are essentially all that survive the review of your beautiful proposal. Of the beautiful cover, wonderful artwork, amazing text, etc., only the "relative strengths, deficiencies, significant weaknesses, and risks supporting proposal evaluation shall be documented in the contract file."

Your proposal gets shredded by the evaluation team into a list of strengths, deficiencies, weaknesses, and risks, and the whole proposal document gets left behind. The only thing that survives is this list.

In practice, the FAR sets the minimum that must be codified in the contract file, and typically agencies embellish it a bit to make it slightly more symmetrical. So, if you have a strength, then you can have a contrasting weakness. If you have a significant strength and you use that terminology, then you could also have a significant weakness. The deficiency means the proposal is so bad it's missing key parts—it's so bad that it's not eligible for award.

Interestingly, risk and weakness are essentially the same thing. It works like this. Every time there's a weakness in the proposal, there's a commensurate risk. Every time there's a risk, there's a commensurate weakness. The two are linked inextricably in this evaluation methodology.

Accordingly, if you have a weakness in a section of your approach because you failed to adequately understand it and adequately address an approach to performing that service or developing that system, the government will say, "Lack of understanding poses a risk to us that we may have to add additional effort. We may have to work harder. We may have to help the contractor through this area, and it's a risk that they may not perform as we expect, perform on schedule, or perform to the anticipated cost."

Weakness and risk are linked inextricably in this evaluation, and the only thing that survives is this list of strengths, weaknesses, risks, and deficiencies.

This list is what moves forward to the evaluation official.

Defining strengths

FAR doesn't define *significant strengths* or *strengths*

Lohfeld Consulting's strength definition—feature of proposal where benefit:

1. Exceeds a contract requirement in a way that is beneficial to the customer

2. Increases [significantly] likelihood of successful contract performance

3. Increases [significantly] likelihood of successful mission accomplishment

4. Is a feature that customer would pay extra to receive

5. Mitigates mission or contract risk

6. Is not neutralized by other bidders, e.g., becomes a discriminator for your bid

To understand and create our strengths, we must have some ground rules around strengths. Since it's the list of strengths that carries the victory, what the heck is a strength?

Well, for a document like the FAR that defines everything so splendidly, the one thing they fail to define is a *strength* or a *significant strength*, yet that's the underpinning of the evaluation methodology.

To define what constitutes a strength, we go to agency source selection guides. I showed two of them to you previously (NASA and DoD) in *Figures 1* and *2* where the government does define strengths. The FAR supplements provide some definition, but not a whole lot.

The best source of information about defining strengths comes from GAO through its writings and decisions in protest cases. As a company, we've gone through this body of knowledge and created for ourselves a practical definition of what constitutes a strength. This is the definition that we use with every client. It's the definition I want you to use in your proposals.

This definition has six parts—all based on the statement that a strength is a *feature of your proposal where the benefit* does xyz.

1. **The first definition is that it's a _feature of your proposal where the benefit_ of that feature is that you can exceed a contract requirement in a way that is beneficial to the customer.**

This is another concept that early in my proposal career I did not understand—that just offering to do the work specified in the contract is like striving to be a C student in college. If you want to be a high-scoring offeror, you must find ways where you can exceed a contract requirement in a way that is beneficial to the customer (for example answering call center calls in 30 seconds when the RFP calls for 60 seconds). Failing to do that leaves you very weak in this concept of evaluation strengths.

So, the first test, the first definition, the first thing we look for in solutioning—is there something in our solution or can we put something in our solution that will exceed the contract requirement in a way that is beneficial to the customer?

2. **The second definition is that it's *a feature in our offer that* increases the likelihood of successful contract performance or significantly increases the likelihood of successful contract performance.**

Contract performance is technical, schedule, cost, quality, reliability, service to the citizen—whatever these measures of performance are going to be—and we take each measure and address it in a thought exercise to say, "What can we put in our offer that increases the likelihood of successful technical performance?"

Typical things that increase the likelihood of successful contract performance include a proven methodology or process, a tool, a management team that's done it before, capital facilities available to support this project without needing to build new ones, etc. All of these arguments can be woven into a proposal to provide evidence that you have a high likelihood of successfully accomplishing the contract's technical, cost, schedule, quality, reliability, service to the citizen, etc. objectives. They're those features that can be scored as strengths.

3. If we take this same concept and now use the Nexus Argument to broaden out the evaluation factors, we can say that a strength is *a feature in our offer that* increases [significantly] the likelihood of successful mission accomplishment (agency mission, safety, lethality, etc.).

Let's look at the agency mission. For example, is there something in a DoD space that increases the lethality of a weapon system, even though that's not specified in the RFP or increases the survivability of troops deployed in the field or systems deployed in a military conflict.

Are there features in our proposal that increase the likelihood of successful mission accomplishment? If there are, they can be evaluated as strengths.

4. Because all the strengths ultimately get traded off against the cost or the price, we ask ourselves, "Is there *a feature in our offer that* the customer would pay extra to receive?" because in the end all these strengths are going to be traded off against the bidder's cost.

To award to other than the lowest priced offer, the selecting official must do that tradeoff and decide that a particular feature or set of features is worth an extra $x million in making that award decision. Are these features in our offer of value to the customer?

In best value procurements, the government can use three different definitions of what constitutes best value. These are:

- You're top of the competition in terms of quality and have the lowest price so your proposal with the top technical score and lowest price constitutes best value to the government, or

- You have the lowest price and all competitors being equal in quality, e.g., the government received proposals from six companies; all offered to do the requested work; all had many great features in their proposals; but your company gave the lowest price so you win. In this definition, lowest price is best value to the government, or

- The government wants to award to other than the lowest priced offer because that company offers features in its proposal that are so valuable to the government that they would pay extra for this set of features—justified by strengths in this proposal. To be strengths, the offered features need to be tangible to the customer and something that they'd pay extra to receive. In this case, an award to other than the lowest priced offer is best value to the government.

5. **Because risk and weakness are linked together, we can look at <u>features that mitigate mission or contract risk</u>, and those features can be scored as strengths.**

If you're mitigating mission or contract risk, you are thereby increasing the likelihood of successful contract performance.

We can approach this from a risk mitigation point of view and look for features in our offer and present them in such a way that they could be scored as evaluation strengths.

We often take every feature that we think will increase risk mitigation and cast them as strengths and vice versa.

6. **Finally, the sixth criteria for us is that the <u>strengths we propose should not be neutralized by other bidders</u>, e.g., if they are not neutralized, then these strengths become a discriminator for your bid.**

It works like this. If we proudly say in a proposal that we are CMMI Level 3, the government at first pass through the proposal will say, "That's a good feature. It increases the likelihood of successful contract performance. We'll score that as a strength."

Then they read the second proposal, and the second offeror is proudly CMMI Level 3, and the third, and so on. When the evaluators finish reviewing all the proposals, they look at them and say, "We've scored everyone a strength for being CMMI Level 3. We should reconsider our scores. Being CMMI Level 3 is not really a strength. That's just the state of the practice."

Accordingly, this apparent strength that the first bidder had is neutralized because all the other bidders say the same thing. To become a discriminator in the final evaluation, the strengths that we propose must not be neutralized by another bidder.

Of course, the converse is truth—we can keep another bidder from having strengths by neutralizing their features that might have been scored as strengths. When we do competitive assessments, we look deeply at how the competitor is going to propose—what's going to be in their solution—and then ask ourselves what we need to do to neutralize what the competitor is doing in their bid to the extent we can anticipate it.

In the final analysis, it's what sets you apart from the competition that wins the day. We're going at the competition one on one to match up strengths to neutralize everything we can about the competitions' proposals.

These six criteria form the body of the definition for what constitutes a strength, and it's a very narrow definition. When we run this definition against proposals, we find lots of features in proposals that companies are terribly proud of, but those features have no merit when it comes to making the final selections.

We had one company tell us, "We have a company cafeteria here, and that's a discriminator." That's not a discriminator because it has nothing to do with increasing the likelihood of successful contract performance. It doesn't increase mission accomplishment for the customer. Is the customer going to pay extra because you have a company cafeteria? Hardly!

By going through this test and using this definition, you can set aside many features in your proposal that take up space, but in the end have no merit and no bearing on the outcome.

Remember—when developing your own proposal, you need to include what you consider to be strengths, even if you know the competition will include similar strengths to neutralize yours—otherwise your evaluation may come back showing weaknesses because of their omission from your proposal.

Use this very narrow six-part definition when you work on your proposals to confirm, "This is what is meaningful. This is what goes forward in the evaluation."

Briefing to SSA

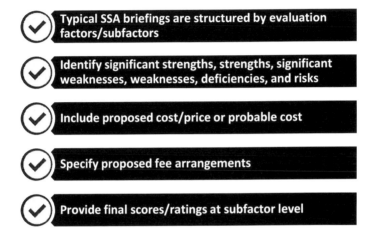

Typical SSA briefings are structured by evaluation factors/subfactors

Identify significant strengths, strengths, significant weaknesses, weaknesses, deficiencies, and risks

Include proposed cost/price or probable cost

Specify proposed fee arrangements

Provide final scores/ratings at subfactor level

Now that we have this firm understanding of what constitutes a strength, what goes forward to the selecting official as prescribed by the FAR are:

- All the factors and subfactors included in the solicitation;

- The strengths, weaknesses, deficiencies, and risks associated with each factor and subfactor;

- The cost or probable cost if it's cost reimbursable or cost priced if it's labor hours or fixed price;

- If there's something interesting in fee arrangements; and

- The final scores of each offeror at the factor and subfactor level.

When you follow this prescription, the typical briefing to an NASA source selection official looks like *Figure 3*.

Briefing: ABC Company

- **Evaluation Factor #1:** Excellent Rating

  ○ Significant Strength #1

  ○ Strength #1

- **Evaluation Factor #2:** Good Rating

  ○ Strength #1

  ○ Weakness #1

- **Risk:** xxx

Evaluated price: $xxx,xxx,xxx

Figure 3. Typical briefing to source selection official.

Figure 3 shows the briefing to the source selection official for the ABC Company. "We the evaluation team looked at evaluation factor #1 and gave it an *excellent* adjectival rating, and the reason we did that is because it has one significant strength and one strength." Well, *excellent* meets the NASA definition of one or more significant strengths (so it meets the strength definition here), no significant weaknesses, and no risks or deficiencies. In NASA parlance, one *significant strength* and one *strength* could get an *excellent* rating.

If we continue and look at evaluation factor #2, it's rated as *good*—that's the middle rating of the five ratings. There's no *significant strength* here, there's a *strength*, and it's offset by a *weakness*. That fits the NASA definition of *good*.

As you begin applying these definitions, you begin to see so clearly that if you don't have multiple strengths, you can't get an *outstanding* rating subordinate to an evaluation factor. If you don't have at least one strength, you can't even get a *good* rating.

The source selection official gets this briefing for the ABC Company, DEF Company, GHI Company, and so on…and is presented with the decision now of "How do I sort this out? How do I pick a winner?"

Source selection decisions

 Selection is a deliberative decision representing SSA's independent judgment

 Adjectival ratings cannot be sole basis for selection decision

 Selection shall be based upon comparative assessment of relative discriminators

 SSA has broad discretion subject only to tests of rationality and consistency with evaluation criteria

Here's a synopsis of the deliberation that goes on with the source selecting official. It is based on FAR 15.308 and numerous GAO protest cases where source selection decisions have been challenged.

- Selection is a deliberative decision representing the _independent judgment_ of the SSA.

- Adjectival ratings cannot be the sole basis for a selection decision. The SSA must evaluate the actual strengths/weaknesses.

- Selection shall be based upon a _comparative assessment of the relative discriminators_ that includes a discussion of the benefits or risks associated with the discriminators of the selected offeror over all other offerors considering all evaluation factors (e.g., past performance factor, cost/price factor, other non-price factors).

- SSA has broad discretion subject only to the tests of _rationality and consistency with the evaluation criteria_ identified in the solicitation.

Let's expand on those four statements.

The selection decision must be an _independent judgement_ of the selecting official. It is not a recommendation that comes from the proposal evaluation team.

Other than certain DoD procurements, the evaluation team is prohibited from making a recommendation. All they do is present the facts—here's how we scored it, here's how we looked at it—and the selecting official will discuss these findings with the evaluation team and can send the evaluation team back to reexamine parts of the proposal if he or she is not satisfied with the findings. But, it's a presentation of data.

The adjectival ratings cannot be the sole basis for the selection decision. The adjectival ratings are more like sign posts along the way to say, "Here's what's coming in the strength and weakness category."

Now you could use the adjectival ratings to make a selection decision if one bidder was blue across all the factors and had lowest price and the others were greens, yellows, or reds across the criteria—then it's pretty straightforward that it was a blowout in the evaluation.

Typically, the colors are much more matched, and you must go beyond the colors to see what constitutes the justifications for those colors and do your tradeoff based on the actual strengths and weaknesses discovered by the evaluation team.

The source selection official's decision is based on a comparison of the relative discriminators. Now here the term *discriminators* says there can't be features that are neutralized by other bidders because then they're not discriminators. Discriminators must survive again the test that we presented earlier. We peel away these features and focus on the discriminators.

Finally, the selection decision must meet a two-part standard. First, it must be consistent with the evaluation criteria, e.g., if you said technical was more important than cost, then when you do that evaluation, you must follow the stated evaluation criteria and not make price more important than technical. Second, the selection decision must be *rational*.

Now I would argue that *rational* is the lowest standard that you can apply to human intellect. You cannot support an irrational decision, a crazy decision, a decision that makes no sense, that can't be explained.

But, if you can explain it, then it's likely to be rational and GAO will uphold that decision.

GAO's job is not to come in and be a Monday morning quarterback reevaluating every decision made by the government's source selection individual. GAO's job is simply to ask was the decision *consistent with the evaluation criteria* and did it appear to be *rational*. If it did, then it meets the test.

It can be a *bad* decision for the agency. It can be a terrible decision because the selecting official doesn't understand the significance and consequence of some of the data that's provided, but as long as the decision is rational and consistent with the evaluation criteria, that decision will stand and it will stand up against protests.

As we go through and work with and teach the source selection decision process, things pop out at us as proposal practitioners that I think fundamentally gore some of the earlier training that we've had in the proposal field.

Takeaways from the evaluation process

1. Your proposal must be prospective

2. Proposals are audited for compliance

3. Proposals are scored based on scoring worksheet

4. Factors and subfactors are the framework for assigning points

5. Strengths neutralized by other bidders won't become discriminators/contribute positively to score

6. Weaknesses and risks are same issue and detract from score

7. Most proposal text is *ho hum*

8. Some proposal sections may not be read or scored

Let's look at some of the takeaways from this proposal evaluation process.

1. Your proposal must be prospective.

Your proposal needs to describe *how* you are going to accomplish the work that's ahead of you and not how great you were in the past. Don't make your proposal a history lesson. It's all about moving forward. That should be completely clear to everybody.

2. **Section L and Section M take on a new meaning in the field of proposal evaluations.**

Proposals are basically audited for compliance to Section L Instructions to Bidders. When you look at proposals, they're not *evaluated* to Section L, they're *audited* for compliance. The structure must be compliant and the content responsive.

Think of it this way. The RFP said provide this, this, and this. When an evaluator opens your proposal, which required certain information be contained within it, that information better be pretty easy to discover. If one of the required pieces of information is missing, you either have a *significant weakness* or a *deficient* proposal. That can be pretty much the end of it. You don't have to go any farther through the proposal as an evaluator. It's game over!

First pass through the proposal is an audit—what we all know as a compliance review. This is what the government will do—look to see if the information is or isn't in your proposal.

3. Proposal scoring doesn't begin until the compliance audit is done.

Now we open Section M Evaluation Criteria in the RFP and build an evaluation worksheet. We go into the proposal wherever we choose to read and read only as much as we need to be able to score the factors and subfactors. In effect, we're going through reading select pieces of the proposal, scoring it, and tying the scores to factors and subfactors.

Section M drives the scoring. High-scoring proposals are designed to resonate with that Section M Evaluation Criteria and put lots of features in the offer that can be scored as strengths. Strengths must be tied to evaluation factors and subfactors and, if not, they won't be scored.

Evaluators don't read our proposals like novels—they read them like encyclopedia entries looking for areas and information to score.

4. Structure the proposal to cross-walk to the evaluation criteria so it's easy to score.

Absolutely—no debate—evaluation factors and subfactors are the framework for presenting your features and their benefits that can be scored as strengths. You can also say, "Well, strengths related to mission accomplishment can be included here too," but the framework for the presentation to the selecting official is always factors and subfactors.

So in a way, our proposal is designed just to produce the results of an evaluation along this framework of factors and subfactors—it's the conveyance of information that populates the scoring template for the evaluation official.

5. **Strengths that are neutralized by other bidders will not become discriminators and will not contribute positively to your score.**

You might have something that's really a nice strength and you think it's really good—but so does everybody else. If you fail to include this strength in your proposal because you figure everyone else will include it anyway, you might get scored as having a weakness in that area— you didn't show that you meet the *state of the practice*.

It's vital that we think about what the other bidders are going to do. We think about what we're going to do, we try to neutralize what our competitors are going to do in the same circumstance, and we hope that they won't neutralize us. If our features/benefits meet the strength criteria, but are neutralized by our competition, they won't contribute positively to our score—but we still need to include them so that we don't get marked down for a weakness in not meeting the state of the practice.

6. **Weaknesses and risks are the same issue and detract from the score.**

For every weakness, there is a corresponding risk. This makes weaknesses in the proposal doubly damaging to our score. If we have a technical weakness, we get down-scored in the technical area of the proposal and separately down-scored in the proposal risk assessment. Because weaknesses and risks are so detrimental to the evaluation and source selection process, we must be extra vigilant to make sure we remove these from our proposals. Failure to do this will quickly lower our score as weaknesses begin to offset our proposed strengths.

7. Most proposal text is ho hum.

By that I mean it doesn't contribute positively or negatively to the score because it has no noteworthy features/benefits. It just drones on with techno-gibberish that fills page after page. Somebody who reads it will say, "It's okay. It's alright. It sets a reasonable approach and I guess they understand it." But there's not one significant finding in the section that can be scored as a strength.

Most of the proposal text that we typically write just drones on and on in page after page of ho hum mediocrity in proposal after proposal. "We're uniquely qualified...we're proud to be your partner..." You can go through 30 pages of a typical proposal before getting past this ho hum text. We need to think about how we manage this text that is never going to be any better than ho hum. Accordingly, don't work so hard polishing this text if it's not going to affect your score.

8. Some proposal sections may never be read or scored because scoring is done from Section M.

If you drive into the proposal using Section M, there are parts of that proposal that evaluators will never ever look at beyond checking for compliance with RFP instructions.

For sure, appendices will never be reviewed (unless the RFP specifically requests them), and yet we see companies wanting to add appendices to proposals because it makes them feel better. This just annoys the evaluators. A lot of executive summaries never get read because they're not point scored, so the evaluators don't go there. There can be sections in the RFP instructions that say, "Provide your configuration management plan," or "Provide xyz," and those items don't show up in the evaluation criteria. You must provide that information to be compliant with the RFP instructions, but it's not going to be scored.

If parts of a proposal are not going to be included in the evaluators' scoring worksheet or unlikely to be scored, e.g., executive summaries or appendices, don't make them the central part of your proposal effort as we often see companies doing.

10 steps to creating high-scoring proposals
A modern perspective on proposal development and what really matters

Part 2 – Rethinking the way we do proposals

10 steps to creating high-scoring proposals

A modern perspective on proposal development and what really matters

Changing the state of the practice

What you learned in the past about writing proposals is no longer good enough

To raise your competitiveness, you must change the way you think about and write proposals

Are you ready to change?

If you embrace this idea of how the government evaluates proposals—what happens behind the curtain—and some of the takeaways from it, then I would contend that much of what we learned (certainly much of what I learned in my early days of writing proposals) is just plain folklore and doesn't really relate to today's approach for writing high-scoring proposals—what we call our modern approach to creating high-scoring proposals.

To raise our competitiveness, we need to change this practice—change the state of the practice within ourselves and within our companies.

Let's look at some of the things we're changing in the way we approach proposals.

10 steps to creating high-scoring proposals
A modern perspective on proposal development and what really matters

Action #1
Design the proposal to be scored, not read

- ✓ 1. Make it easy for evaluators to audit
- ✓ 2. Make it easy to score
- ✓ 3. Make strengths pop off the page so they're easy to find
- ✓ 4. Visually communicate strengths in addition to text
- ✓ 5. Features must explicitly meet strengths/benefit criteria
- ✓ 6. Use feature/benefit/proof construct to present strengths

The first action that we take is designing the proposal to be scored, not to be read. This is a fundamental difference. You'll see people that say, "I've got to read it from beginning to end. It has to be read like a novel and tell a story."

But proposals are not novels. They're not great literature. They're more like an encyclopedia with topic after topic written in a certain way that can be scored. Here are six concrete ways to design a proposal to be scored, not read.

10 steps to creating high-scoring proposals
A modern perspective on proposal development and what really matters

1. **Make it easy for the evaluators to audit.**

Enable the evaluators to audit your proposal easily for compliance and responsiveness with Sections L, C, J, etc.—wherever these instructions reside.

2. **Make it easy to score.**

Do this by building your own scoring worksheet using Section M and navigating into the proposal, checking to see if you can find all the stuff that you need to be able to score it. If you can't easily find this information, then you failed to create a proposal that's easy to score.

3. **Make the strengths pop off the page so they are easy to find.**

We've had the government come back through debriefings and say to the bidder (our clients), "We are so grateful for the way you presented strengths so they pop off the page. You made it so easy for us to evaluate your proposal in contrast to other companies that make it so hard and difficult. They hide the information. They don't even address what we need. You made it really easy to score."

4. **Visually communicate your strengths in addition to using text.**

So here we need to communicate for the proposal *skimmers*, and I'll talk more about that further on in the book. Evaluators skim proposals, and they look for things that pop off the page. You must communicate information visually.

5. **Features must explicitly meet the strengths/benefit criteria.**

Features must explicitly meet the strengths/benefit criteria that I discussed earlier in this book, and if they don't, those features have little chance of being scored as a strength. You must make it clear to the evaluators why and how each feature meets the strengths/benefit criteria.

6. **Use feature/benefit/proof construct to present strengths.**

Every time we present a feature, we link to it the benefits so evaluators can see directly that we're meeting this benefit criteria. Then we try to provide proof—some evidence that we didn't just make it up for the proposal—that it's real and has some credibility to it.

Always think in this construct of feature/benefit/ proof. Please don't say that, "I have a feature/ benefit/proof table and I've done my job," because most of the time when we see that in a proposal, it's full of gibberish and excessive abbreviations. By making these feature/benefit/proof tables so poorly done, what we're really doing is training the evaluators to skip over them.

If you have a feature/benefit/proof, then it needs to be developed in the proposal and explained in such a way that it can be scored as a strength. Additionally, it must be presented in a way so that it pops off the page and it's easy to define and easy for the evaluators to score.

Design proposals to be scored, not read. That's the first action.

Action #2

Use our *strength-based solutioning* approach to create high-scoring proposals

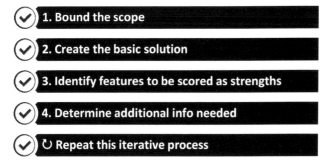

1. Bound the scope
2. Create the basic solution
3. Identify features to be scored as strengths
4. Determine additional info needed
↻ Repeat this iterative process

Let's use this concept that we created—*strength-based solutioning*—to create high-scoring proposals. The merit of each proposal's *solution* resides in its strengths, and if we embrace this concept early in the proposal development process during solutioning, we will create a much richer solution—a higher-scoring solution—and with a high-scoring solution, we can create a high-scoring proposal.

10 steps to creating high-scoring proposals
A modern perspective on proposal development and what really matters

Our four-step methodology works like this.

1. Bound the scope.

Discuss and bound the scope of the RFP section that you are addressing (discuss Sections L, M, C, as applicable). Let's gather the team of subject matter experts (SMEs) who are going to work on this solution, select a specific section of the proposal, and *bound the scope* as we say in engineering.

Discuss the scope as a team and agree on what it really means. When the RFP says, "Describe your capability…," what does the word *capability* really mean? Do they want us to describe the whole universe or just some narrow piece of it? Let's bound the scope of this section. Let's all agree on what it means and create our understanding of it.

2. Create a basic solution.

Define and discuss your proposed solution and how it meets RFP requirements. If we understand what the requirements are—and the better we understand the requirements—the better our solution will be. Let's create a basic solution that provides an approach to doing the required work and then look at that solution and ask the question outlined in step 3 below—what's in that basic solution that the customer will care about in such a way that they can score it as a strength?

3. Identify features to be scored as strengths.

Identify features of your solution where the benefit meets our strengths test. Do we have features in our solution that exceed a contract requirement in a way that's beneficial to the customer? Do we have features that increase the likelihood of success? If we do, then good for us! If we don't, then let's go back to the drawing board and create a richer solution that incorporates these features that can be scored as strengths.

4. Determine additional information needed.

Determine what else you need to know to develop a solution that's rich in features that can be scored as strengths. When the technical team starts to whine and say, "This is too hard!" because they don't know this or that or we didn't tell them this, then let's make a list of what we didn't tell them. Let's make a list of what they need to know and then go get that information. You'd be amazed at what you can find if you know what you're looking for. Once we have this list of questions and needed information, let's get the answers, come back a few days later, and go through this iterative process again.

This four-step methodology becomes a loop when we add in the new information and then go back through discussing the scope, reviewing the basic solution, embellishing the list of features that can be scored as strengths—making critically sure that our strengths meet the definitional test. We document those defined strengths and assign them to the appropriate evaluation factors and subfactors using a feature/benefit/proof construct.

By going through this iterative process, we are well on our way to creating a high-scoring solution, and this is done by defining what constitutes a high-scoring solution and challenging the experts in our organizations to design our high-scoring solution.

Every high-scoring proposal begins by creating a high-scoring solution, so let's put our effort where it matters and create an *outstanding* or *excellent* solution that is rich in features that can be scored as strengths.

Action #3
Draft your briefing to the SSA

✓ **1. Set a strengths budget**

✓ **2. Draft source selection briefing**

✓ **3. Identify any weaknesses**

✓ **4. Collect *strengths observed versus strengths bid* metric**

✓ **5. Build a company strengths registry**

It's all about strengths. The best solution is the one with the best—and maybe the most—strengths with no weaknesses. If the briefing to the source selection official is so critically important—the end goal, what we want to accomplish—then let's design our proposal to produce a very successful source selection briefing.

Let's set a strengths budget for every evaluation factor and subfactor and innovate your solution until you have engineered in enough strengths to win. You saw in the source selection guides' definitions that you can't get a blue score in a NASA procurement evaluation without having one or more significant strengths. So, if we're bidding on a NASA RFP, that factor better have at least two significant strengths or we're not working hard enough to get us where we need to be. If it's DoD, it must have at least two strengths to get a top score. Yet most companies go through their proposal development process ignoring the concept of creating a strength budget. Let's bring that to our game. For every evaluated proposal section, we're going to set out a budget of what we think we need to win. The more you do this, the better you'll get at it.

Draft your own source selection briefing by evaluation factor and subfactor, and identify all your proposed strengths. Let's draft the source selection statement along this journey in capture and then address it again during the proposal development phase. Every time we do this, we find things that we put in the source selection statement that failed to show up in the proposal. If we're drafting the source selection statement along the journey, we can use that to drive features back into the proposal that would never have been there otherwise.

Don't forget the topic of *weaknesses.* Carefully go through your offer and solution as a Devil's Advocate to identify any weaknesses. When you identify weaknesses, develop ways to mitigate them, and add that to your proposal because that risk mitigation can be scored as a strength.

Now if we're creating a strengths budget and populating the proposal with strengths, then we need to have a performance metric that captures from our post-award debrief how many strengths the government evaluators observed. Accordingly, we create a metric called *strengths observed versus strengths bid*. For example, we bid seven strengths in management and the government evaluators observed three. What happened to the other four?

Over time, we want to drive this observed versus bid strengths metrics to unity as a metric, but we also want to do a root cause analysis that says, "They missed four strengths. Maybe these features weren't actually strengths. Maybe we misunderstood what they were looking for. Maybe we didn't present our features/benefits/proof points in a way that the evaluators could find them.

There's something wrong if our observed versus bid strengths metric doesn't move towards unity. Begin collecting metrics on the number of proposed strengths observed versus strengths bid and drive this ratio to 1:1.

Finally, because many of the strengths you develop are *reusable*, we tell our clients to begin building a company strengths registry. Use it just like a playbook in sports. We ran this play on third down last time, and we got seven yards. Let's run it again.

Let's do the same thing with the strength registry so that when we begin to develop our solutions for various procurements, down the road the third or fourth time we've been through a solutioning exercise we'll have a substantive strengths registry that we can use as a cheat sheet for subsequent bids. Strengths are reusable—absolutely.

Action #4
Think of proposals like artwork – built in three layers

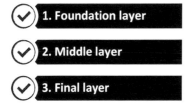

I like to tell companies to think about proposals like great artwork. When you talk to an artist, they'll tell you that they paint great portraits in layers.

They begin with a *foundation layer*. They take their canvas, they sketch out the proportions and perspective, they put in some construction lines, and they basically rough out the shape and the size the way they want it.

Then they create this *middle layer* where they're adding in the color and the texture, and the palette is used to make this picture come to life—to make it interesting and engaging.

They then have a *final layer*—the varnish layer—where they put a varnish over the painting to bring out the luster and the pigments, to unify the painting, to make it communicate better to the audience, and to preserve it.

When we look at proposals, we do them in much the same way. We have a foundational layer, which is a compliant structure with responsive content. We get the document all shaped out and we have a basic proposal.

If we were to submit that basic proposal to the government, they would evaluate it and say, "This is a good proposal—no weaknesses, no deficiencies, no strengths either, but that's a good proposal." It's not an excellent or outstanding proposal. It's just a good proposal—sort of middle of the road. The C *student* if you will.

1. **Foundation layer synopsis**

   - Develop compliant organizational structure

   - Make proposal responsive to RFP requirements

   - Outcome—basic proposal with no weaknesses or deficiencies

But then we create our middle layer in proposals where we take all these features that we believe will be scored as strengths, bundle them up with their benefits and proof, and layer them into the appropriate sections in the proposal.

Two things come about from doing that. When we do it, our proposal becomes rich in features that can be scored as strengths—after all we're trying to design a high-scoring proposal.

Because we put so much emphasis on benefits, the proposal begins to take on a different tone. It becomes a proposal that's all about the customer and all about how we are going to make the customer successful—and less about how proud we are of our pedigree as a bidder.

The middle layer makes the proposal enduring to the customer.

2. Middle layer synopsis

- Allocate strengths (features/benefits/proofs) to sections where they will get the most points

- All benefits are focused on exceeding contract requirements, increasing likelihood of successful contract performance or accomplishing customer mission, or reducing performance risk

- Outcome—a compelling customer-focused proposal rich in features that will be scored as strengths

Lastly, just like artwork, we have a final layer where we go through our proposal, make it easy to evaluate, make sure it communicates visually, and ensure it's well written and a document that we can be proud of.

10 steps to creating high-scoring proposals
A modern perspective on proposal development and what really matters

I like this concept of artwork—of the three layers—because it ties so well to the strength-based solutioning directive. The foundation layer is the basic solution. It's steps one and two in strength-based solutioning—define the scope, get it organized, and provide a basic response.

Step three in strength-based solutioning—identifying all the features, benefits, and proofs—brings in all these features that turn this sketch into artwork.

The final layer, which I'll talk about in Action #9 *Establish a standard of excellence for your proposals,* is this idea that the proposal must communicate easily to the evaluators so they can score us well.

3. **Final layer synopsis**

- Easy to evaluate, communicates visually, and well-written

- Outcome—high-scoring proposal

Think of artwork and think of strength-based solutioning—the two tie nicely together.

Action #5

Put your proposal effort where it matters

- ✓ **1. Focus on parts that will be scored**
- ✓ **2. Stop discussing *themes* and call them *strengths***
- ✓ **3. Use executive summaries to showcase strengths**
- ✓ **4. Stop polishing text when it can't get a higher score**
- ✓ **5. Increase the number and quality of strengths**

Put your proposal effort where it matters. Not all parts of the proposal will be read or scored equally, so if we're going to focus on pieces, let's focus on the pieces that will be scored.

We proved this in a study with a team of 40 individuals who facilitate the evaluation of large contracts/proposals for the government. We did the study with an agreement that we wouldn't disclose the company, the procurements, or the people involved, but we could talk freely about what we learned from the study.

Think about a company like MITRE or Aerospace Corp.—that's the kind of service they provided. The first question we asked these 40 facilitators was, "What did you think of our proposal themes?" Forty to zero they responded, "What's a theme?"

"A theme? A theme! You know the thing we lock ourselves in a conference room to create, debate, deliberate, shout, and eat pizza and discuss for 3 days and then come out thinking that we've conquered the world."

They said back to us, "You don't understand what we do! We're going through your proposals looking for *strengths*. A *theme* doesn't show up in the FAR or in our evaluation guidance."

This idea of proposal themes is invisible to the evaluators. Stop talking about *themes* and call them *strengths*. I'm on a personal campaign to drive the word *theme* out of our lexicon. It may have served us well years ago, but today it's all about strengths. Themes are invisible.

"Well if you didn't get the themes, what did you think of our eye-watering executive summary? That proposal piece we labored over for days. It's pure poetry telling you everything we're going to do for you."

Half of the facilitators came back and said, "We didn't read it."

"Why didn't you read it?"

10 steps to creating high-scoring proposals
A modern perspective on proposal development and what really matters

"Well, because we didn't have to score it. So why am I taking on extra work? You've got to understand! I've got a kid and a dog, and I want to go home for little league soccer, and I need to mow the lawn, and I'm going to school at night, and I'm not making proposal evaluation my career. If I didn't have to score it, I didn't read it!"

Well, for us executive summaries are *okay* to include in a proposal because they're a place to put a rollup of all these features that we want the evaluators to score as strengths. So, the executive summary can be like a scoring guide to say in an abridged way, "If you read the proposal, here are all the great features you're going to discover that should be evaluated as strengths." Just building that executive summary/scoring guide is about all that it's worth.

So, don't make your executive summaries labors of love that go on for days. Find out what your features are that can be scored as strengths, roll them up to the front of each section of the proposal, then roll them up to the executive summary, and you're pretty much done.

Most proposal text will be scored as either *Satisfactory* or *Deficient*. It's ho hum. It did the job—nothing particularly meritorious here, nothing noteworthy. So, if it is only ever going to be scored as satisfactory, why are you on the seventh iteration of that text? Why didn't you say at iteration three, "Good enough is good enough" and put it in the box? We go on and on polishing proposal sections until the response time is exhausted when good enough is probably good enough. Stop polishing proposal text when it cannot receive a higher grade.

The key here is that if you want to increase your proposal score, then put your effort where it really matters. Put it into engineering features into your solution that can be scored as strengths, and then convey them effectively in the proposal.

Government evaluators are reverse engineering our proposals into their scoring sheets and capturing the strengths. Increasing the number and quality of proposed strengths will take a proposal from good to great!

Action #6
Review proposals the way your customer does

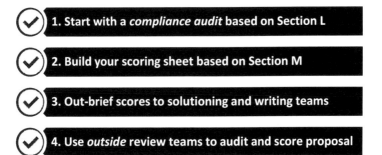

1. Start with a *compliance audit* based on Section L

2. Build your scoring sheet based on Section M

3. Out-brief scores to solutioning and writing teams

4. Use *outside* review teams to audit and score proposal

Somewhere along the road in industry, proposal reviews (color teams) just skidded off the track and became editorial reviews. Proposal teams break up the proposal into sections, and folks carefully read those sections like editors—not an activity designed to produce high-scoring proposals. I contend that typical color team reviews largely miss the mark.

The way we do proposal reviews is different. We don't have a pink team, red team, gold team, platinum team, plutonium team, and so on.

We conduct three reviews. The first review is called the *first draft compliance review*. The second review is a *scoring review*. After all, what really matters is that we're putting numbers on the scoreboard—so let's do a scoring review. The third review is the *quality review*.

Again, it kind of follows this idea of layers—the first draft compliance review (do we have all the required elements in our proposal where they are supposed to be), then the scoring review (do we have all the features with supporting benefits and proof points in the proposal that can be scored as strengths), and then the quality review (have we added our quality/luster/varnish layer and are we getting this proposal looking the way we want it).

The first pass through, we do a compliance audit like the government does. We're rigorous about it just as everybody has been since the beginning of time. If the proposal is not compliant and responsive to the RFP, game over.

The scoring review is different from color team reviews. Color team reviews generally begin with Section L, and the two review types will give you very different results. We determine the sections we need to read to score the proposal (don't read the proposal like a novel—it's more like reading the encyclopedia).

We build a scoring worksheet on a spreadsheet based on Section M and make it look like one the government would put together.

We bring together an evaluation team that includes Lohfeld consultants plus some of our client representatives, and we brief them about how to evaluate the proposal. Individually, we review the proposal looking for content to use to complete our scoring worksheets, and then as a team we build out an evaluation document with our scoring results. Next, we out-brief the scoring results to the solutioning and proposal team.

This scoring review process has caused more than one proposal team to go back and restructure their proposal.

Let me give you an example of how this worked. We were working with a major client on a high-value deal, and they were at red team. They wanted us to do a scoring review following our methodology, but we overlaid our methodology with theirs. We told them, "Do your traditional red team review, and then we want to come to the briefing of the red team and brief your team after you do your internal red team outbrief. For this review, we want everybody who's involved in solutioning and everybody who's involved with writing and all the reviewers in the room."

So, they kicked off their red team review. They critiqued their proposal in what you would recognize as a traditional review—add this bullet here, change this paragraph, it would be a little stronger if you said *happy* rather than *glad*—and this kind of editorial discussion went on with a few insights added to the proposal.

10 steps to creating high-scoring proposals
A modern perspective on proposal development and what really matters

Well, the proposal team was sitting around the table giving each other high fives and saying, "You know we're going to be done with this puppy in about 2 days. We'll polish it off and we'll have a long weekend."

Then we briefed. We said, "Well, factor one technical— we reviewed it and there's not a strength in sight, so we gave it a *good* rating, but not an *excellent* or *outstanding* rating. We read the management section and couldn't find one strength, and found a similar lack of strengths through the rest of the sections. What you are doing with this red team/editorial review is striving to create a well-written mediocre proposal. You could polish this rock until the end of time, and it would never be better than mediocre from a scoring point of view."

When the solutioning team and the proposal team heard this, their jaws dropped. They stopped the review and pulled the whole solutioning team back to re-solution their offer. They incorporated their revised solution with the features, benefits, and proof points that could be scored as strengths into the proposal, and the proposal gods were shining on them because the government gave a 3-week extension. The second time we went through our scoring review, they had taken the proposal from good to great and the outcome was a $500 million win for that team that they would never have had if they hadn't followed this methodology.

10 steps to creating high-scoring proposals
A modern perspective on proposal development and what really matters

We're rethinking the way companies conduct proposal reviews and building scoring into them, and it's changing the game for our clients.

Action #7
Make proposals easy to evaluate

✓ **1. Highlight strengths so they pop off the page**

✓ **2. Showcase strengths in introductions to major sections**

✓ **3. Present strengths to stand out in sections**

✓ **4. Present strengths as feature/benefit/proof**

✓ **5. Show features/benefits meet our *strengths test***

✓ **6. Structure proposal to cross-walk to evaluation criteria**

Make proposals easy to evaluate. I can't stress this enough.

Evaluating proposals is hard work, and the evaluators often are not experts to the level that you are in the topics they are evaluating. I don't think many evaluators volunteer to be locked away in a room reading and evaluating proposals. It's not a glamorous or sought-after assignment. We need to make evaluators' tasks easier for them and design our proposal so they are easier to evaluate.

Additionally, evaluators get tired, they get worn out, they get distracted, and believe me if you've read the same topic three times by three different offerors, the one you read last is in real trouble because you can't concentrate on it.

You read the first with interest, the second with some interest, and by the third you're zoned out and you might have 25 more proposals to go. It is so important that we make our proposals easy to evaluate. When we do this, we've had government evaluators come back and thank our clients for writing proposals that were so easy to score.

Make sure you cross walk the evaluation criteria into the structure of your proposal. Ensure an evaluator can easily navigate into your proposal and find the information they need to score your offer.

So often, the proposal instructions fail to call out all the topics that are listed in the evaluation criteria, so as the proposal designer we have to add these evaluation topics into the structure in a way that they are easily found and easily scored. Remember, proposal evaluators do not want to make evaluating your proposal their life's work. If they can't find what they're looking for easily, it will never be evaluated. Get the structure right so they can find your features that should be scored as strengths.

Next, make the strengths stand out and make them easy for the evaluators to find using their scoring sheets—like the ones you created for your internal evaluations.

Many evaluators don't know if a feature is a strength or not, so you must help them along in their decision process. You should lead them to the conclusion that your feature should be scored as a strength, and the best way to do this is to point out the benefit the government will receive from this feature. Make sure your benefits meet the benefits test listed in Part 1 of this book. Add in some proof that what you are claiming as a benefit is real, not something made up by people in the proposal war room just to fill in white space in your book.

Always make your strength argument using the feature/benefit/proof construct we discussed in Action #1, and you will have a customer that comes back and says, "Thank you very much for helping us understand that each feature is a strength."

Finally, highlight strengths so they're easy to recognize and pop off the page. Whatever you do, don't bury your strengths deep in some paragraph that a tired reader may skip over. Make your strengths stand out.

A word of caution here. Don't get carried away with feature/benefit/proof tables. Most of these tables are poorly done and use so many abbreviations that they are unintelligible to the reader, and often the features listed in the table don't meet the strength test. Poorly done tables train the evaluators to skip over them because these tables are not easily understood. Again, remember that evaluators are not going to work that hard to evaluate your proposal. If a feature is really a strength, then lay out the argument well and make it easy to find on the page.

We'll talk more about this under visual communications techniques in Action #8.

Summarize significant strengths in the executive summary, and showcase them in introductions to major sections. Present strengths so they stand out in each section and show that your features/benefits meet the test to be scored as evaluation strengths as we discussed earlier in Part 1 of this book.

Action #8
Communicate your message visually

1. Use visual communications to convey strengths

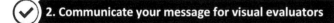
2. Communicate your message for visual evaluators

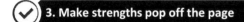
3. Make strengths pop off the page

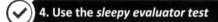
4. Use the *sleepy evaluator test*

Visual communications is one of my favorite topics. We use the term *visual communications* as opposed to *graphics* because what we are doing is taking our message about strengths and trying to communicate those strengths *visually* to the reviewers. This may sound like a subtle distinction between graphics and visual communications, but it is more significant than that. Visual communications begins by listing the strengths we want to communicate and then figuring out how to convey them visually. It does not begin by selecting a graphic and trying to shoehorn your features into it.

We learned the importance of visual communications through conducting numerous review exercises. If you take a team of really smart people, and you ask them to evaluate a proposal and watch how they evaluate it, one third of the team will go through that proposal, read the text, and skip over every figure in the proposal. They'll skip over the data in every table, and they'll just read the words. They're *text readers*, and they don't see the graphics on the page, the visual communications on the page, or the tables on the page.

You can prove this to yourself. Watch them evaluate. At about five pages into the proposal, have everyone close their laptops or turn the proposal face down on the table. Then ask how many people in the room can tell you what was in the graphic on the second page. They may give you some generalization, and then you begin to probe beyond that to see how many of them really *saw* what was in the graphic.

You'll be shocked at how few can come back to you and tell you what's there.

Another third of the evaluators can tell in detail what was in the figures and tables. They are typically the engineers or the scientists. The highly technical people tend to focus on data and will skip the words. They'll look at the flow diagrams and the data in the tables, and they will evaluate your proposal based on what they perceive visually. You have the left brain/right brain thing going on here.

We use visual communications to convey your strengths to evaluators who don't read text.

10 steps to creating high-scoring proposals
A modern perspective on proposal development and what really matters

We also know that the more proposals the government evaluators review, the more important visual communications becomes. As evaluators get tired, they default to visual communications. They skim the proposal looking for features that pop off the page, or key words in paragraphs, or action captions under tables and figures. This makes it doubly important that we design proposals with good visual communications.

To communicate effectively, we must communicate our message across two frequencies. One is text, and one is visual. To accomplish this vitally important visual communication, our strengths must pop off the page. We should use ways to highlight them using bold text, italics, pull quotes, colors, or icons—whatever you want from an artistic point of view. You have to use some visual technique so evaluators can find your strengths easily. Communicate strengths in section headers, graphics, action captions, figures, and tables.

We do a test for visual communications that we call the *sleepy evaluator test*. We take the proposal and give our reviewers 10 seconds per page to evaluate it. You cannot read a page in 10 seconds. You must evaluate it visually—look at the graphics, look at the tables, check out the pull quotes. Flip through the document—10 seconds per page—and score the proposal.

You'll be amazed in doing this. There's not one point you can put on the scoreboard if visual communications failed in the proposal. Visual communications fails either fundamentally because there's no content that's noteworthy to be scored, or the proposal developers failed to present it effectively. The proposal is full of graphics, but there's no *visual communications*.

Use the 10 seconds/sleepy evaluator test—this becomes more important the more proposals someone has to evaluate, and some of these procurements are evaluating 100+ proposal submissions. Can you imagine? The evaluators just go through them quickly and separate them into two piles. The regret letters go out early and it's all done visually.

Design your proposals for two communications channels—the visual and the textual.

Action #9
Establish a standard of excellence for your proposals

1. Compliant structure

2. Responsive content

3. Customer focused

4. Compelling and feature rich

5. Easy to evaluate

6. Good visual communications

7. Well written

Establish a standard of excellence for your proposals. This is what we teach our clients. We have seven quality measures that we apply to every proposal.

1. Compliant structure

Our proposal is compliant with the instructions (Section L), evaluation criteria (Section M), statement of work/PWS (Section C), and any other relevant sections of the RFP. No one could argue with this, but many proposals fail to meet this basic quality measure.

2. Responsive content

Each proposal section fully addresses what the RFP requires. When it says in the RFP, "Describe your approach to staffing this project," don't start with this arm waving, "We're national. We recruit on seven continents. We're best of breed…" Skip all of this mumbo jumbo out of the corporate boilerplate. Talk about what they really asked for. If they asked you to describe your approach to staffing the project, tell them how you're going to staff that project. Merely having the right headings and sub-headings isn't enough. Your content must address what is requested. It must be responsive.

3. Customer focused

Emphasis is on what the customer wants, not on how important the bidder is. If we're doing our job with feature/benefit/proof as a construct, and we're talking about the benefits to the customer, the proposal becomes very customer-centric. It's all about making the customer a success.

Customers always want to hear about how you are going to make them a success and how you can help them achieve their mission objective, as well as the benefits they will get from your offer. They are not particularly interested in hearing about how important your company is or that you claim to be *best of breed*. Kill those self-gratifying proposal words, and focus your proposal on how you are going to make the customer a success.

4. Compelling and feature rich

Our proposal includes features and benefits with substantiating proofs that are apparent as strengths. For us, a compelling proposal is one that can be scored highly because it is rich in features that can be scored as evaluation strengths. The more strengths you offer and the better these strengths are, the more compelling you offer will be.

5. Easy to evaluate

Evaluators can easily score our proposal because it includes cross references and compliance matrices and maps back to the evaluation criteria. Evaluators get tired. Make the evaluation easy for them.

6. Good visual communications

Our proposal is attractive with sufficient white space and uses graphics, icons, tables, callout boxes, and other techniques to highlight features and benefits and break up dense text. Proposal reviewers may be nodding off as they're reading our proposal, so make sure they can clearly identify our features/benefits/proofs as strengths.

7. Well written

Our proposal uses active voice, maintains a consistent tense and conventions, and avoids vague or empty words as well as unsubstantiated bragging. Drive out the empty content and words that writers love to insert into

10 steps to creating high-scoring proposals
A modern perspective on proposal development and what really matters

proposals that make them feel good and are meaningless to the evaluators. Review our article on *100 words that kill your proposals* as well as the other related articles included at the end of this book.

Seven quality measures studies

As Lohfeld Consulting Vice President Lisa Pafe writes in her white paper, *Win rates double with seven quality measures* (https://goo.gl/qQxiC8), we tested our quality standards on review assignments for six of our customers across 23 proposals, which allowed ample opportunity to assess results. With the cooperation of these customers, we reviewed these proposals and participated in a minimum of two color team reviews each to further refine the approach and make iterative improvement of the scoresheets, customized to the specifics of each solicitation and each of our customers.

We obtained customer feedback as to the scoresheet effectiveness and ease of use, as well as whether they planned to incorporate the methodology into their processes. Customers responded favorably, stating that the scoresheet template is easily customized and tailored to each RFP. The resulting recommendations are specific and actionable, and therefore proposal teams can create effective recovery plans. Rather than saying, "This is no good," the resulting recommendations detail how to actually fix the document in alignment with the government evaluator perspective.

10 steps to creating high-scoring proposals
A modern perspective on proposal development and what really matters

Proof of success

We analyzed results by comparing how these customers fared in terms of win rates before implementation and after process improvement through use of the seven quality measures in proposal reviews. This analysis required customer cooperation as they had to agree to *open their kimonos* in order to reveal their average win rate and to provide proposal outcomes. The proof is in the results. Participating customers saw their win rates double upon implementing the resulting recommendations for color team recovery as shown in *Figure 4* below.

Client requirement	Quantitative results
Better proposal review methodology	Provided six customers with improved methodologies focused on how government evaluates bids
Actionable results for proposal recovery	Applied seven quality measures to improved proposal recovery for 23 bids
Improved proposal ratings	Average scores increased from 1.67 (4-point scale) to 3.94, a 136% improvement
Increased win rates	Win rates improved from an average of 32% to 76% (either won or won on technical)

Figure 4. Proof of seven quality measures success.

These outcomes are well above the industry average of overall company win rates for new and re-bid business ranging from 30–50%.

We did something similar with another major firm, and all we did was say, "Set up these quality measures. Show people what they are. Then start measuring the quality of your proposals in the final proposal review that you do, and put the scores up on the wall so people can see them." Over the course of a dozen proposals, their scores began trending upward, and their win rate trended up with a 30% increase. Not bad for seven quality measures.

Measure all proposals against your standard—what gets measured gets improved.

Action #10
Improve your lessons-learned exercise

- Raise the importance of lessons-learned exercises
- Analyze results after receiving debrief
- Employ *strengths observed versus strengths bid* metric
- Plan corrective actions for future bids
- Analyze lessons learned by customer, division, business unit, capture/proposal manager
- Maintain statistics and use them to continually improve capture and proposal processes

Lessons learned for most companies are generally deplorable. They're really lessons *relearned*.

Hold two lessons-learned meetings—one after proposal submission (within 1 week) and one after you get your government debrief. Examine what worked and what didn't work in both your capture and your proposal processes.

We hold a final lessons-learned review after the government has made the award, has debriefed our client, and we have an outcome.

These debriefs and their accompanying lessons learned need to be analyzed. Let's take seriously this metric of *strengths observed versus strengths bid*. How are we doing? Understand why there was a difference in strengths observed versus strengths bid. Plan corrective actions to improve future bids. If we're not measuring this, we can't expect to improve.

We need to baseline. We need to drive towards a better metric. How many strengths did we bid? Did we win? As you begin collecting this data, you begin to see profiles by customer, profiles for different divisions and business units in your company, and profiles for different capture and proposal managers.

Archive the results of your lessons-learned exercises, and use the archived lessons-learned information to in-brief the next team bidding to a particular customer or on a similar job. There's a lot of useful, actionable information contained in debriefs.

Let's make lessons learned a central part of our process and strive to continually improve the scoreability of our proposals. Keep lessons-learned statistics at the business unit level and use them to continually improve your capture and proposal processes.

Final thoughts – can you change?

I think about science and history and how beliefs evolve over time. Think about astronomy and Aristotle…and then Copernicus…and then Kepler. Aristotle was convinced that everything in the universe revolved around the earth because the earth was much too heavy to move. His views about the universe were largely wrong, but they survived for 1,000 years because there was no measurable *data* to disprove his beliefs.

Copernicus and Kepler advanced science because they had real data that disproved Aristotle's views about the motions of the planets. Even with real data, changing beliefs was hard. It took a long time, and new views were met with great resistance.

I tell customers that all of us learned to do proposals the *old way*. When I say this, there are always a couple of people in the room that pipe up and say, "Well, I'm too young to have learned the old way, so I'm buying in to what you're saying."

The problem for us as proposal practitioners is that management learned to do things the *old way*, and they learned a lot of stuff that's wrong. But they're the managers, and our job is to convince them through intellectual argument and through examples and data that there's a better way.

In science when you can convince someone that what they believed is not valid, you become world renowned as a scientist. Every one of the famous scientists has debunked some prior belief, published it, and the world moved in a new direction.

What we find so hard here in the science of proposals is that there's huge resistance within companies that want to do it the old way, and we constantly work at them. For each of you reading this book, we need you to drive this same message forward for your teams and embrace this *modern* perspective on proposal management and what really matters within the proposal process.

10 steps to creating high-scoring proposals
A modern perspective on proposal development and what really matters

Part 3 – Q&A

10 steps to creating high-scoring proposals

A modern perspective on proposal development and what really matters

Q&A

In this Q&A section, I'd like to answer some questions that we've received from folks regarding the way the government evaluates proposals and about our 10 steps to creating high-scoring proposals.

Question: How do we keep our review teams from turning our proposal reviews into *editorial reviews* when we give them scoring sheets and nobody completes the scoring sheets?

Bob's answer: I think this comes down to basic training where reviewers learn how important it is to identify strengths and weaknesses. If the reviewers don't understand how important this exercise is, then, as you suggest, they will drift off the task and start *editing* the proposal.

Every reviewer wants to edit and rewrite the proposal, so to keep the emphasis focused on evaluating the proposal for strengths and weaknesses, we task evaluators to just *score* the proposal and not offer suggestions to rewrite it. Leave the editing exercise up to the editors and focus the reviewers on scoring the proposal by identifying the strengths and weaknesses. This is what puts points on the scoreboard.

10 steps to creating high-scoring proposals
A modern perspective on proposal development and what really matters

Question: How do I create a strengths registry? What should it look like?

Bob's answer: Strengths are reusable just like plays in a football game. Every professional sports team has a play book, and every proposal team should have a strengths registry.

Organize the strengths registry by typical evaluation criteria. Let's have major sections in the registry that include technical, management, past performance, transition plan, small business subcontracting plan, etc. Subordinate to these major sections, you could have types of work, e.g., software development, hardware manufacturing, products, types of professional services, etc.

Now go through your proposal and take each strength you bid and place it in the appropriate sections of the strength registry. Do this for each of your submitted proposals. You might want to annotate the registry entry with what proposal you pulled the strength from. You can do this after your proposal was submitted and then update it after you get your debrief.

Keep your registry as a living document, and add to it every time you do a proposal. Every time you do a proposal, look back at the strengths registry to see if there are strengths you can reuse. In time, you will get very good at creating strengths and can offer strengths that you know have scored well.

Question: Our proposals must be awful! We get so many Evaluation Notices (ENs) each time we submit a proposal. What should we do?

Bob's answer: ENs are a good thing, and you should be more worried that you didn't get many or that they are trivial. The government is giving you a chance to improve your proposal, and you want to take full advantage of them.

The government is not allowed to mislead you, so when they say you missed the mark in some section of your proposal, take the guidance at face value and respond accordingly.

Question: We often have insufficient time to develop our proposal strengths, and our SMEs are too busy dealing with our client and our subcontractors and vendors in putting together our basic approach to identify strengths. How can I identify our strengths and our discriminators?

Bob's answer: Start early and begin building out strengths during capture. Even though you don't have the evaluation factors and subfactors, you can do this by thinking about your value proposition. What are you offering to do that will help the client accomplish their mission, increase the likelihood of successful contract performance, exceed a contract requirement in a way that is beneficial to the customer, etc. Document this in a draft briefing to the source selection official, and review this draft when you review capture progress.

If you are making progress and are understanding customer requirements, goals, needs, and objectives, you can create a high-scoring solution. If not, then you are just *tracking* the procurement and must do more than that to win.

Start early, draft your value proposition and features you want to offer, and these will become the strengths in your bid.

Question: How do we know what features the client will see as beneficial to them?

Bob's answer: Best informed wins. The better you understand the needs, goals, objectives, preferences, and biases of the client, the better you will be able to develop features in your offer that can be scored as strengths.

Don't just spring these features on the customer for the first time when you submit your proposal. Try to get some validation from the customer during capture that your features are really strengths.

I've seen instances where a company offered an innovative solution, and the government scored it as *high risk*. Perhaps if the company had socialized the idea with the government before the RFP was released, they could have modified their solution to eliminate the perceived risk.

I've also seen instances where we previewed a solution with the government and were told we didn't understand their requirement correctly. The government customer went on to say that if we changed our approach and added these features to it, it would be just what they needed. It doesn't get any better than to have the customer help design your solution.

Try to take the risk out of your bid by validating your solution.

Question: In reference to the Nexus Argument, if we include benefits in our proposal that are not directly applicable to the RFP requirements, but are kind of tangential in nature, are things like that scored or just set aside as tie-breaker items by the evaluators?

Bob's answer: That is a good point. They might be scored and that would be preferential, but keeping them as a tie-breaker is ok too. The important thing here is that when you develop your solution, think about it more broadly than just solutioning to the factors and subfactors...think about the customer's mission and include that in your solution effort.

Question: We're used to putting features/benefits tables in our proposals. Are *features* essentially the same thing as *strengths*? Should we start using strengths/benefits tables instead of features/
benefits tables?

Bob's answer: I like the idea of calling them *strengths* and then describing in some level of detail each feature, its associated benefit, and some evidence to substantiate your claim. You might use titles like *Features that can be scored as strengths* or *Solution Strengths*—whatever you are comfortable with.

One important consideration here is that whatever strengths you present in the table must really be strengths. If you fill up a table with poorly thought out features that you claim to be strengths, you will most certainly be training the evaluators to skip over all your tables and not review them.

If you call it a strength, it really has to be one.

10 steps to creating high-scoring proposals
A modern perspective on proposal development and what really matters

Question: How many strengths should we budget to include in our bid?

Bob's answer: I think the best way to do this is to look back at proposals you have submitted to this customer. Look at how many strengths you had when you won and how many you had when you lost. This might give you some idea of what it takes to win.

If you have not bid to this customer before, you might look at similar bids and then file a request under the Freedom of Information Act (FOIA) for the Source Selection Decision Document. This is the document where all the strengths and weaknesses are discussed for the various bidders and how they were considered in the award decision. You might be able to get this document or a redacted version of the document, which can give you more insight into how many strengths are needed to win.

If none of this information is available, then just make a guess as a starting point and tell your solutioners to try to exceed your number. One thing is certain, if you don't set a target for the number of strengths you need, then any solution will meet your requirement.

Question: Are there different outputs from the three different types of proposal reviews you suggest?

Bob's answer: Each review focuses on making your proposal better.

The first one is a compliance and responsiveness review. Here we are looking for areas of the RFP that we failed to address or address adequately. These could be because we failed to include them in our proposal outline, failed to adequately address them, or misunderstood the scope of what was being asked in the RFP. In any case, the first review focuses on driving out weaknesses in the proposal, and most weaknesses come from failure to address an RFP requirement.

The second review focuses on finding strengths in the many pages of proposal text. It is the strengths that put points on the scoreboard, and most proposals drone on without a strength in sight, and most solutions are just adequate and meet the minimum RFP requirements. We want to make sure we are proposing a solution that is rich in features that can be scored as strengths. If we conduct the second review focused on strengths, then we can improve our solution and improve the scoring of our proposal. The second review is all about improving strengths.

The third review is about how well we communicated our solution to the customer. Is it well written? Does it communicate visually as well as textually? Is it easy to evaluate? In this final review, we pull it all together using our Seven Quality Measures to make sure we have a compliant, responsive, compelling offer and that we communicate it effectively to the customer.

Question: At what point in the development of the proposal document should I do each of the three types of reviews—compliance review, scoring review, and quality review?

Bob's answer: This is a great question, and we have experimented with scheduling these reviews at different times with different degrees of success.

I like doing the compliance review at the same time you would do your pink team review. You have to have a fairly complete proposal to do this, so if your book is only partially done, then this review can't provide guidance other than to say your proposal needs to be more complete.

The second review is done when you would normally do your red team review. The proposal has to be complete and in pretty good shape. You want to do this review late enough in the proposal development lifecycle that you have a pretty good book, but not so late that you can't make significant changes to your solution.

You can also rerun the compliance review concurrently with the scoring review since it is generally failures in compliance that create most proposal weaknesses.

The final review can be run when you would normally do your gold team review. This review is your overall proposal quality check. If you have done a good job reworking the proposal following each of the earlier reviews, you should have no weaknesses and lots of strengths—so the final challenge is to polish the proposal so it communicates your message effectively to the customer.

Question: Can you give me some examples of strengths that could be reusable and included in a company strengths registry? (I thought we were supposed to develop new text for every proposal and not reuse material from previous proposals.)

Bob's answer: Some examples of strengths are:

- Methodologies or processes that you have previously used with significant results.

- Tools that you use to do the work that, again, provide significant improvements in outcomes.

- Facilities that you have that are operational and can be used to manufacture your proposed solution.

- New technology that you are introducing that gives you a competitive advantage.

Question: By the time most of our proposals are finished and delivered, everyone is so tired and can't stand each other. Do you have some suggestions for how I can get the lessons learned information I need for our archives?

Bob's answer: I like to send an email to all the BD, capture, proposal, and executive participants and ask them to think back about the life of this bid beginning from when they first learned about it through delivery of the proposal and then tell us in short statements what worked well, what could have gone better, and what recommendations they might offer to make the next bid more efficient and effective. I tell them that we will consolidate the comments into a lessons-learned document and strip out any personally identifying information so the comments can be submitted on a not-for-attribution basis.

After we get all the comments pulled together and edited, we have a pizza lunch for all the stakeholders and go over what we learned.

The final step is to save the lessons learned in a corporate archive so the next time we bid to that customer, we'll have the benefit of all our lessons learned at the beginning of our journey.

10 steps to creating high-scoring proposals
A modern perspective on proposal development and what really matters

Question: Usually it's our capture manager who ends up developing our proposal solutions in our company. Who is the best person to be developing our proposal solutions? What's the best way to do this?

Bob's answer: The capture manager owns the solution, and the proposal manager is charged with getting that solution into a high-scoring book.

These two people need to work as a team, and this team should be commissioned when the deal is still in capture. If they work together, they can start building proposal artifacts before the RFP is released and, hopefully, with more lead time to develop these, you will have a better solution requiring fewer people to create the proposal once the RFP is released.

Question: Can you address *risks* and how we might be able to use all the strengths that we've identified in our proposal for some sort of risk mitigation table?

Bob's answer: Driving risk out of the proposal is just another way of identifying features that increase the likelihood of successful contract performance.

Every feature that increases the likelihood of successful contract performance can be cast as a risk mitigation action and vice versa. Doing these together in the solutioning sessions will help unify the proposal strengths.

When you have to address risks in the proposal, start by looking at each strength you have and postulating a risk which that strength mitigates. If you build your risks this way, you are accentuating the features in your offer that should be scored as strengths when you address risks.

Question: Who are the most *qualified* people in our company to participate in the proposal reviews you suggest we do?

Bob's answer: We like people who have good proposal experience, have a solid understanding of the work you are proposing, and have gone through a training class in how to evaluate proposals the way we do.

For companies interested in learning this methodology, we teach an onsite class using our review templates and techniques and apply the review to one of your proposals. I personally believe the training is transformative for the reviewers, and they will never review a proposal the same way they did before.

We also find it very cost effective for our clients to have one of our consulting staff lead their proposal reviews because, as an outsider, we bring an independent perspective to the proposal review and it is easier for us to *tell it like it is*.

10 steps to creating high-scoring proposals
A modern perspective on proposal development and what really matters

Part 4 – Related articles

Related articles

The following published articles support the concepts we've discussed in this book. You can find more on our blog at http://www.LohfeldConsulting.com/blog

7 questions to answer when making bid/no-bid decisions

By Bob Lohfeld

Did you ever wonder why some companies have higher win rates than others?

You might think at first that these companies have smarter people who are better trained at proposal writing, better proposal development processes, and maybe newer tools to help them write winning proposals.

While all of these reasons may be valid, there are often more subtle reasons that have less to do with people, process, and technology and more to do with executive decision-making and the health of their new business pipeline. Let me explain why this is the case.

Picking losers over winners

Making good bid decisions is the quickest way to raise your company's win rate. It is far quicker than hiring better people, improving poor proposal processes, or investing in capture and proposal technology. In fact, making better bid decisions brings about an immediate improvement in win rate and, as an added bonus, lowers your annual cost of proposal development.

Contrary to popular belief, the key to making good bid decisions is not picking the deals in your pipeline that you are going to win, but instead, it is discarding the deals that you are going to lose.

If you rank order deals in your new business pipeline from highest to lowest win probability and ignore for a moment the value of the deals, you would certainly bid deals at the top of your list first, ahead of all the deals at the bottom.

If you bid only the deals at the high end of your list, you will enjoy a high overall win rate. As you move down your list bidding more deals, your overall win rate will decline.

Bid decision dilemmas

It should be obvious that to raise your company win rate, you must stop bidding deals that you have little or no chance of winning.

Then why, if this is so obvious, is it so hard for executives to no-bid these deals? Basically, there are two reasons.

First, the need to win more revenue trumps the need to make good bid decisions. In most instances, the desire to win is so dominant that decision-makers will ignore obvious no-bid indicators such as the client doesn't know our company, we know nothing about the work other than what is in the RFP, we don't have a technical solution, and we don't know who we are competing against. All these are clear indicators that winning this deal is a long shot, yet deals like this are bid every day. As one executive summed it up, "If we don't bid, we can't win."

What he didn't say was, "If we bid all the long shots, we are going to spend a lot more money and lose a lot."

The second reason is that most executives don't have a good alternative if they choose to no-bid. If they don't bid, then their proposal resources will have to sit idly by waiting for the next RFP to come in the door and with their anemic new business pipeline, they could be waiting a long time. Most executives rationalize that it is better to bid something, no matter how low the win probability, than to bid nothing at all.

This can become a vicious cycle for companies because they get so caught up in bidding long shots that they don't have time to stop and fix the systemic problems that got them in this situation in the first place.

Making informed bid decisions

Knowing what losing bids look like can be very insightful when it comes to making your next bid decision. To help identify the losers, I encourage companies to make a bid scorecard for deals they have

10 steps to creating high-scoring proposals
A modern perspective on proposal development and what really matters

bid. The scorecard will not tell you whether or not to bid, but it should tell you when the deal is really right for you and when you are reaching for a deal that is a long shot.

Here's how you can build your own scorecard.

Your scorecard should list the top seven factors that you believe are leading indicators of whether or not you will win a bid. You can have more than seven, but to get started, let's keep it simple and use just seven. If you don't know what these factors should be, then use the list below to get started. You can always change them or add to them as you get more experience doing this.

1. Do we understand the customer's mission and the work to be performed?

2. Do we have a solution that will help the customer achieve its mission and contract objectives?

3. Do we have a relationship with this customer through meetings or prior contract performance?

4. Do we know whom we are competing against and can we beat them?

5. Do we have a teaming strategy and can we get the right subcontractors?

6. Do we know what price we need to bid to win and can we achieve it profitably?

7. Do we have a compelling win strategy?

Next, gather up data from approximately 20 bids that you did over some reasonable period of time. Don't go back more than 2 years because memories tend to get fuzzy when you try to answer the above questions on deals done a long time ago. Plus, your company's capabilities change over time so old history may not be a good predictor of future results.

For each bid, find the answers to the above questions and color code each answer based on how you would have scored them when you made the bid decision. I like to use four colors—blue, green, yellow, and red—to score each question. For example, in the first question about how well you understood the customer's mission and the work to be performed, score the answer *blue* if you deeply understood the mission, had met with the customer on multiple occasions, and were fully confident that you understood the requirement. If this was a pop-up bid and you had never met the customer or done work for that agency, then score the answer *red*.

Separate your bid scorecards into categories based on the type of procurement. For example, full and open bids, task order bids, set-aside bids, etc. Forget the bids where you were a subcontractor since winning those deals is more about the prime contractor than your role as the subcontractor.

Next, divide your bid scorecards in each category into groups based on bid outcome. You should have three groups—winners, losers, and bids where the outcome has not yet been decided.

I like to stick the bid scorecards up on the wall so you can see the color scores by procurement type and outcome grouping. You will likely see more *blues* and *greens* on the scorecards for the deals that you won and more *reds* and *yellows* for the deals that you lost. This should be particularly true for the single award, full and open bids. Don't let data from some of the GWAC bids confuse your findings. For example, deals like Seaport-e and 8(a) Stars have almost no losers, so they really belong in a separate category all to themselves.

From the scorecards, you should begin to see profiles emerge for the deals you lost as well as deals you won. The scorecards will likely reveal that there were some deals on the wall you should never have bid. What you want to see are the characteristics of deals that are losers and deals that are winners.

As you collect more data, you can build a mathematical model to predict your win probability. These kinds of models translate your color scores into numerical values and add weighting factors to each of the questions in your bid model. The process of making these models is called multivariate regression analysis, and the more data you collect, the more confidence you will have in your model predicting statistical outcomes.

Making bid decisions should become a quantitative exercise designed to maximize the likelihood of achieving your overall revenue objective. The value of deals in your bid portfolio and their win probability are keys to computing the likelihood of achieving this objective.

Not every new deal will match your past findings, but more insight into recent past experience can help executives make better-informed, objective bid decisions. The more you use this kind of analysis with color scores or quantitative models, the more comfortable your executives will become with making no-bid decisions and discarding deals you can't win.

Fixing pipeline health

It is easier to no-bid a deal if there is a better new business opportunity in your pipeline. If this is not the case, then you have a pipeline health problem that needs to be fixed. Your pipeline should be rich in opportunities to pursue, and your decision to pursue them should be limited by the in-house and consulting resources you can afford to devote to writing good proposals.

To help ensure you have alternatives to bid, divide your bid list into two categories—an A list and B list. The A list deals are the deals you intend to bid and are working hard to get positioned to win. Your B list deals are the ones you would like to bid, but don't have the resources to bid them unless one of the deals on the A list falls by the wayside.

Inevitably, some deals on the A list will not be bid because the procurement is delayed or cancelled or maybe you will decide that your probability of winning is too low. In this instance, you will want to move a deal up from your B list to your A list to replace the deal that you are not bidding.

If you don't have enough deals in your pipeline to do this and your pipeline looks more like a pipe drip, then more energy needs to go into market research and deal qualification. On the other hand, don't let the market research team overpopulate your new business pipeline with deals you can't explore.

Going overboard with new deals will turn your pipeline into a pipe dream.

Summing it up

One of the CEO's at a company we work closely with told me his win rate was up 20% this year. I asked him how he did it and expected him to say it was due to the outstanding capture and proposal services we provided, but he didn't say that.

10 steps to creating high-scoring proposals
A modern perspective on proposal development and what really matters

He said simply, "I stopped chasing losers." It sounds easy to do, but often it is a hard lesson to learn.

From WashingtonTechnology.com.

10 steps to creating high-scoring proposals
A modern perspective on proposal development and what really matters

Take your proposal from good to great in 30 minutes

By Bob Lohfeld

Thirty minutes is all the time you need to redirect the writing of a mediocre proposal and put it on a clear path to victory. In this article, I'll explain how to use this simple yet effective technique.

Proposal mediocrity

We had just finished a Red Team review on a typical 100-page proposal. The proposal manager instructed the review team on how to do an effective Red Team review. The reviewers had done an excellent job reviewing the proposal and documenting their comments electronically.

They briefed the proposal team, and it was clear what needed to be done. While the proposal team could easily turn the comments in 48 hours and make the repairs needed to the proposal, there was a sense that the proposal just didn't come across as a winner.

The proposal team knew they had done an admirable job building a compliant proposal outline that was easily traceable to the RFP instructions and evaluation criteria. The review team confirmed that the proposal text was, for the most part, compliant with the RFP. They pointed out where additional content was needed and where text and graphics could be improved, and they provided additional content that would help make the proposal more responsive to the requirements.

Yet, the team still had an uneasy feeling that it takes more to win than building a compliant, responsive bid.

We have talked in previous articles about the 7 factors we use to build winning proposals; the first 2 of these factors are compliance and responsiveness. But these alone are not sufficient to win.

A proposal must provide a compelling offer, rich in features that can be scored as strengths, and this is where our proposal was falling short. It was at best, a *ho-hum*, compliant, responsive bid without any distinguishing characteristics that would make it a winner. Enthusiasm lagged as no one had any brilliant ideas as to the path forward.

I'm sure you have seen this situation many times before. The team is demoralized, but still committed to hunker down and go the distance to make this the best proposal they can.

10 steps to creating high-scoring proposals
A modern perspective on proposal development and what really matters

Getting the proposal back on track

I explained to the team that writing a great proposal is often similar to creating a great oil painting. The great masters like Rembrandt and Rubens always created their oil paintings in three distinct layers—the foundation layer, the middle layer, and the final glaze layer.

I explained to the team that like artwork, they had created a foundation layer with a compliant proposal structure. They were midway through completing the middle layer, which is the responsive text that fills in all the voids in the proposal structure, and they were now ready to begin the final layer that provides the highlights and luster that is so recognizable in great art.

In proposals, the winning layer is the features of your offer that the evaluators can score as strengths. You must highlight each strength in the appropriate place in your proposal in order to receive the maximum score. And, of course, you do not want to have any weaknesses.

For government proposals, strengths must meet the *strength test*—features that exceed a contract requirement in a way that is beneficial to the government or increase the likelihood of mission or contract accomplishment. These strengths must be unique to your offer, or at least not offered by all bidders. Strengths are always tied to the evaluation factors or subfactors.

10 steps to creating high-scoring proposals
A modern perspective on proposal development and what really matters

Building the final layer of the proposal

I instructed the proposal team and the reviewers to create an email message addressed to me, the capture manager, and the proposal manager. Next, write four headers in the email—one for each evaluation factor.

In this case, the evaluation factors were Technical Approach, Management Plan, Transition Plan, and Past Performance.

Next, I asked them to simulate writing their own briefing to the source selection official (SSO). The briefing had to follow the RFP evaluation factors and include each of the major strengths or significant strengths of the offer tied to the appropriate evaluation factor.

They were not constrained by what was written in the proposal. Instead, I asked them to write down all the reasons (strengths) that their offer should be selected for this award. This heads-down, independent exercise gave them 5 minutes to list all the features they want the SSO to find. They had 5 minutes to write down as many noteworthy strengths as possible cross-walked to the evaluation factors. Everyone was done within the 5-minute timeline.

Next, we did a roll call of each member of the proposal review and writing teams asking them to tell us what strengths they had written for the first evaluation factor. We had 20 people on the call, so in the next 5 minutes, all

20 debriefed their strengths for the first factor. We then went to the next evaluation factor and continued until all four evaluation factors were briefed.

With the final roll call, the team had identified about 100 features that could potentially be scored as strengths. Yet, 80% of these identified strengths had not made it into the proposal.

This situation is not unusual because the writing process often focuses only on compliance and responsiveness to the RFP instructions. Writers respond to the RFP instructions rather than the strengths that are essential to winning. Many participants identified the same strengths under an evaluation factor. These are likely to be the strengths that the evaluators will find as well.

To wrap up the process, I asked the participants to take an additional 5 minutes to ensure every strength had a well-identified feature with a corresponding benefit offered to the customer and at least one proof point that substantiated the claim. Each strength must include a feature/benefit/proof construct to receive a maximum score, so I asked everyone to make sure their email followed that structure.

At the 30-minute mark, I asked everyone to hit the *Send* key, and the exercise was done. I told them the proposal team would review each suggested strength, deliberate whether it met the strength test, and then place it in the proposal where each would receive the highest score.

Within 30 minutes, the morale of the proposal and review team had changed. Everyone could see the final layer of the proposal taking shape and bringing the luster and brightness that was promised. The final layer transformed a dull, *ho-hum*, compliant, responsive bid into a winning proposal.

Of course, the proposal team still had more to do to polish this bid into a winning proposal. However, the trajectory of the bid had been lifted from a mediocre response to a winning offer in just 30 minutes.

From WashingtonTechnology.com.

10 steps to creating high-scoring proposals
A modern perspective on proposal development and what really matters

What makes your bid a winner or a loser?

By Bob Lohfeld

I was asked to review a major best-value bid for a firm that was notified they had lost and wanted to protest.

Emotions were running high, and they were making all sorts of allegations about the government not wanting them to win. I asked to see their debriefing file, and what I discovered was surprising—at least to me.

Like many companies, they failed to understand why companies lose and what it takes to win.

Why do you write proposals?

Always remember that proposals are written for one purpose—to convey the information the government evaluators need to select your company over others in the competition. Proposals are not written to show the government how smart you are or to brag about your company history. They are not written to showcase your team members or to boast about your world-class best practices.

Proposals are written to score *points* with the evaluators.

10 steps to creating high-scoring proposals
A modern perspective on proposal development and what really matters

When evaluators tally your *points*, they are generally not talking about a numerical score, but instead the number of strengths and weaknesses they give your proposal when they read and score it.

The real purpose of your proposal is to convey your strengths to the evaluation team and show that your offer has no weaknesses.

Strengths are features in your proposal that either increase the likelihood of successful contract performance or offer to exceed a contract requirement in a way that is beneficial to the government. Some RFPs define additional characteristics for strengths, but in general, this is a pretty good definition for a proposal evaluation strength.

For features to be scored as strengths, they need to be unique to your proposal or unique to several proposals because if every bidder proposes the same feature, then that feature will not be scored as a strength.

Your job as a capture manager and/or proposal manager is to ensure your proposal is rich in strengths and that each of your strengths gets conveyed clearly to the evaluation committee, who will in turn brief those strengths to the source selection official (SSO).

10 steps to creating high-scoring proposals
A modern perspective on proposal development and what really matters

To have a winning proposal, you must do more than just respond to the proposal instructions and evaluation criteria. Your proposal must be compelling—rich in strengths—and have no weaknesses.

Picking the losers

I have always maintained that the government picks losers first, and the last bidder left standing is the winner in the source selection process. Here's how it works.

The proposal evaluation team briefs the SSO on the strengths, weaknesses, deficiencies, and price of each offer. Some agencies include significant strengths and significant weaknesses in the briefing. With this information, the SSO performs an independent determination of which offer represents the best value to the government and documents these findings in the contract file.

In practice, the SSO eliminates offers from further consideration based on their deficiencies, weaknesses, lack of strengths, and price. If your bid has one or more deficiencies, it is game over. Your bid is set aside as a loser, and you lost in the SSO's first evaluation pass.

If your proposal has no deficiencies, but has multiple weaknesses not offset by multiple strengths, you will be in the next round of losers selected. If your proposal has no deficiencies or weaknesses, but has fewer strengths compared to other bidders, you will be next in line as a loser.

If your price is too high, you will be moved to the next group of losers. After all, there is a price above which the government will not pay no matter how good your proposal is.

This process of selecting losers continues until only a few bidders are left in the race. At this point, the SSO may look beyond the number of strengths. The SSO examines the merit of each strength, and compares the value of these strengths and your bid price with other finalists.

Bidders continue to be deselected until just one bidder remains. In the final analysis, the last bidder left standing is the winner.

Disgruntled bidder

The proposal that I reviewed was clearly a loser despite being well written and having no deficiencies. As we would say in the trade of writing professional proposals, it was compliant and responsive.

What it lacked was a compelling technical approach. The disgruntled bidder scored only two strengths in their technical approach, while other bidders scored eight to ten strengths in the same sections.

I told the disgruntled bidder they failed to engineer evaluation strengths into their technical approach, and that is what cost them the win.

A sound technical approach with no weaknesses is necessary, but not sufficient to win. They now understand that they must outscore their competitors, and in the end, it is all about evaluation strengths.

From WashingtonTechnology.com.

How bad are your proposals?

Only 15% of companies said their proposals were always compliant, responsive, and compelling

By Bob Lohfeld

In a previous *Washington Technology* article, *6 ways your proposal can fail*, I wrote about a company that submitted a less-than-professional proposal and wondered how pervasive this problem really is. After all, as professional proposal managers, how bad can our proposals really be?

All professional proposal managers strive to make every proposal compliant, responsive, and compelling, yet a recent presentation reinforced my assessment that only about 15% of the firms bidding on U.S. government contracts consistently achieve these fundamental objectives.

In a GovCon Business Development Weekly webinar hosted by Deltek's Michael Hackmer, I discussed four fundamentals for creating a winning proposal. The first three fundamentals comprise creating a compliant, responsive, and compelling proposal. We polled the 150 webinar participants from a cross-section of small to large government contractors and asked them to rate how well their proposals did in achieving those three objectives.

What we learned was surprising. Only 15% said their proposals were always compliant, responsive, and compelling. That leave 85% saying their proposals fell short of these primary objectives.

A deeper look at the results showed that only one third said their proposals were generally compliant, responsive, and compelling. That still left about half the respondents saying their proposals generally failed to meet these objectives.

This is certainly cause for concern since we all know that the best way to lose evaluation points immediately is to submit a proposal that is not compliant, responsive, or compelling. What's so troubling about these statistics is that these firms may have proposed wonderful solutions or service offerings, but because of the quality of their proposals, they likely didn't win.

The fourth objective for creating winning proposals is developing a well-defined solution or service offering that is rich in features that deliver real benefits to the customer—and most importantly, developing the solution and features before starting to write the proposal. In the software business, this is analogous to saying, "Let's design before we start coding."

10 steps to creating high-scoring proposals
A modern perspective on proposal development and what really matters

Having a good solution or a well-defined service offering is a prerequisite to writing a good proposal, yet in my experience many companies start writing before actually defining their solution or service offering. The webinar survey data supports my observations about solution-first writing. About one third of respondents do no solution development before writing. They just start writing and hope that a solution emerges. Clearly, these companies have work to do to improve their basic capture and proposal development processes.

The final question we asked was about the use of capture and proposal processes. Good proposals are the result of well-defined capture and proposal processes. Good processes will consistently produce better proposals, improve win rates, and reduce proposal development costs—yet only half the respondents said they had defined capture and proposal processes.

No wonder so many companies' proposals fail. Having little or no process, writing before developing a solution, and failing to meet the compliant, compelling, and responsive standards is a sure way to lose.

I probably should have asked one more question, "How many respondents want to improve their proposal win rate?" But, I guess the answer is obvious since that's why they participated in the first place.

From WashingtonTechnology.com.

3 keys to creating winning proposals – a defined and efficient process is essential to success

By Bob Lohfeld

Creating winning proposals is not the same as writing a proposal. Anyone can write a proposal for government work, given enough time and resources. However, only one bidder writes the winning proposal. The best proposals have three things in common:

1. They are directed and written by talented people experienced at writing proposals.

2. They follow a similar, defined process.

3. They are designed in an environment that creates proposals efficiently.

Your capture and proposal managers bring necessary skills to plan, staff, lead, and control your capture campaign and develop your competitive proposal. They work as a team and understand each member's role. The capture manager leads the campaign, and the proposal manager comes in before a request for proposals is released to focus on developing the proposal.

10 steps to creating high-scoring proposals
A modern perspective on proposal development and what really matters

This team knows that the first step is developing a winning solution. During the capture phase and pre-proposal phases, they work together to:

- Create a clear win strategy. Win strategies derive from a competitive assessment that focuses on your competitors' strengths and weaknesses. Understanding these enable you to create a win strategy that highlights your strengths and mitigates your weaknesses while neutralizing your competitors' strengths and accentuating their weaknesses.

- Develop and document the solution. Solution development begins during the pursuit phase as a separate exercise from writing the proposal. Create and document your solution, complete design trade-offs, conduct reviews and approve the solution before writing the technical and management response.

- Build in significant strengths. Every winning proposal is rich in features that evaluators will assess as proposal strengths. These features are engineered into your proposed solution to show that your approach increases your likelihood of successful performance or that your solution exceeds a requirement in a way that is beneficial to the government customer. Those strengths are explained to the selecting official along with your price and used as the basis to differentiate competitors and justify selection of the winner.

Although each proposal is different, the process used to create winning proposals generally has these characteristics.

- Early proposal planning and development. Great proposals begin during the pursuit stage well in advance of the final RFP. Pre-proposal activities are funded, a proposal manager and support staff are assigned, and proposal development begins. Draft text and graphics are created in anticipation of the RFP. That includes the technical description of your solution, management organization structure and management plans, past-performance summaries, key employees' resumes, management and technical processes, and data calls to team members. Portions of significant proposals and any proposal designated as must-win should be substantially written before RFP release.

- A compliant, easy-to-evaluate proposal structure. Winning proposals always comply with the RFP. The proposal structure follows RFP instructions and evaluated information is easily found. Good proposal structures are developed early, validated independently, and approved before authors begin writing. The structure must be well crafted because it serves as the foundation for the proposal.

- Proposal sections designed before writing. Each section is designed using either an annotated outline technique or a storyboard.

- Responsive and compelling proposal text. Text responds completely to the RFP, assertions are substantiated by evidence—not rhetoric—and benefits are clear to the customer. The proposal is written compellingly and is easy to read and score.

Winning proposals are developed in an environment with a well-established proposal development process, using appropriate tools to facilitate the process. A collaborative workspace for archiving capture data and managing proposal development, workflows, and version control is essential. Virtual meeting tools are vital for reviewing documents and hosting discussions. Publishing tools bring efficiency to the process. Up-to-date company databases of past-performance summaries, personnel resumes, prewritten proposal material, proposal graphics, and past proposals are equally helpful.

From WashingtonTechnology.com.

What the government won't tell you about your proposal

By Bob Lohfeld

Congratulations, your proposal has made competitive range, and the government has contacted you to discuss your offer. What the government will and won't tell you in these discussions can be a surprise to the unprepared bidder, but sophisticated players know the rules and what to expect.

First, it is important to know if your dialogue with the government is a discussion or a clarification. There is a difference, and it is important to which type of communication is being requested.

Discussions are a formal part of the federal procurement process that allows the government to engage in a substantive dialogue with offerors. They occur after the competitive range determination.

If you engage in discussions, a meaningful two-way exchange of information, then you are entitled to revise any part of your proposal you desire—unless, of course, the government tells you otherwise.

If you engage in clarifications, responding to requests from the government to clarify what you wrote, then you are not entitled to change your proposal. Always confirm which type of communication is being requested if you're not clear.

Discussions need not be equal

When agencies enter into discussion with offerors, they do not have to treat offerors equally. For example, an agency can have discussions with one offeror about its price proposal and not discuss any other sections of that offeror's proposal. For a second offeror in the competitive range for the same procurement, the agency has no obligation to discuss that offeror's price proposal even though they did with the first. However, when conducting exchanges with offerors, agency personnel may not "engage in conduct that…favors one offeror over another," (Federal Acquisition Regulation (FAR) 15.306(e)(1)); in particular, agencies may not engage in what amounts to disparate treatment of competing offerors.

Discussions need not be comprehensive

The government has no obligation to discuss weaknesses in your proposal, even though you might presume that is the purpose of discussions. FAR 15.306(d)(3)) is skillfully written so that when conducting discussions with offerors in the competitive range, those discussions include "at a minimum…deficiencies, significant weaknesses, and adverse past performance information to which the offeror has not yet had an opportunity to respond."

Agencies are not required to afford offerors all-encompassing discussions or to discuss every aspect of a proposal that receives less than the maximum score. Agencies are not required to advise an offeror of a minor weakness that is not considered significant, even when the weakness subsequently becomes a determinative factor in choosing between two closely ranked proposals.

If the agency determines that your proposal is full of weaknesses that are not deemed significant, it does not need to discuss them.

Discussions are not intended to provide the whole truth about how the agency scored your proposal.

Discussions must be meaningful

When an agency engages in discussions with an offeror, the discussions must be meaningful—sufficiently detailed to lead an offeror into proposal areas requiring amplifications or revisions that materially enhance its potential for receiving the award. The government may help you rid your proposal of significant weaknesses and deficiencies—assuming you made competitive range— but don't expect it to lead you to eliminate weaknesses in your offer.

10 steps to creating high-scoring proposals
A modern perspective on proposal development and what really matters

If you understand the discussion rules, you'll know that discussions focus on remedying significant weaknesses in your proposal, not on leveling the playing field. Be prepared to correct these significant weaknesses—and any other hidden weaknesses when you submit your revised final proposal.

From WashingtonTechnology.com.

3 steps to improving your proposals – break the cycle of relearning key lessons each time around

By Bob Lohfeld

No proposal is ever perfect. Every company executive wishes he or she had just a few more days to tweak the last sections. But, after the proposal goes out the door, it is time to reflect on what did or did not go well in the proposal process and what could have been done to improve the outcome. A review of lessons learned is a valuable step in improving proposal development efficiency and raising your win probability on the next bid.

Surprisingly, not all companies do such reviews. Even more surprisingly, many companies that do them repeatedly make the same mistakes. The review should follow the same process after every significant proposal. The process has these three fundamental steps.

1. Gather data

Give the proposal team a few days to settle back into its normal operations before trying to collect information about the last proposal. People need time to reflect—but not so much time that they forget what they learned. One or two weeks is typically the right time frame to begin data collection.

Start the data collection process by selecting the participants and inviting them to join in the review. Participants should include the proposal team, technical and management contributors, executive team, and subcontractors. Congratulate the team on the successful proposal delivery and set expectations for the review. Ask the participants to reflect on the proposal process and their experience on the proposal team. This will enable them to share their perspective on what they could have done differently to improve the process and the proposal.

Designate someone to be the recipient of all the comments and ask each participant to send comments to that person. Ask for comments covering the full life cycle of procurement, not just the proposal development phase. You will want comments about opportunity qualification, pursuit and pre-proposal phases in addition to the proposal development phase. For each phase, each participant should address three fundamental questions: what went well, what didn't go well, and how activities could have been done differently to improve the process and the proposal.

10 steps to creating high-scoring proposals
A modern perspective on proposal development and what really matters

2. Analyze data

Begin by sorting the comments along the procurement timeline. For example, group all comments dealing with pre-proposal activities together and then sort those into subcategories by comment type: what worked well, what didn't and how to improve. Combine redundant or similar comments and edit out comments about an individual's performance or comments that might become career-limiting expressions of personal dissatisfaction. Those are personnel issues to be dealt with separately and are not part of a process improvement review.

Use a three-column table to show the analysis results. The columns are symptoms, root causes, and recommendations. Most comments will describe symptoms, not the root cause of the problem. For example, writers who consistently miss deadlines could be a symptom of several different root causes. Perhaps they are overworked and fully billable during the day, the corporate culture doesn't enforce deadlines, or they never had proposal training. Whatever the reasons, getting at the root cause is critical because treating symptoms just masks the real problems.

This is the hardest part of the analysis because most people treat the symptoms without ever understanding the root cause of the problems. We need to fix what is broken, not just treat the symptoms—and of course, we want to preserve what is working and be open to accepting improvement suggestions.

3. Learn from mistakes

Brief corporate management and the proposal team with the results of the analysis. Give them time to understand the findings and accept the recommendations. Improvement requires careful changes to processes, better training for participants and investments in better technology. Implementing them requires consensus and a road map for change.

If you conduct your lessons learned review correctly and after every proposal, you can break the cycle of relearning the same lessons after each major proposal.

From WashingtonTechnology.com.

5 steps to winning proposals

By Bob Lohfeld

I'm amazed at how few companies present good, compelling technical solutions in their proposals. The reason is probably that their technical teams don't know what constitutes a good proposal solution.

In this article, I'm going to describe the process we use to ensure we develop solutions that will score well when reviewed by government proposal evaluators. Here's how we do it.

Step 1 – Understand the requirement

The first step in engineering is to understand the requirement. I don't mean to speak down to you since this seems pretty obvious, but I've read a lot of proposals where the technical team misunderstood the requirement or misinterpreted the intent of the government's RFP.

To make sure everyone understands the requirement, we do a structured walkthrough of the requirement with the technical team. We discuss what is in the statement of work (SOW), the relevant attachments to the RFP, the proposal instructions, and the proposal evaluation criteria.

Let's also make sure we agree on what is not part of the requirement. As engineers might say, "Let's bound the problem." Otherwise, our solution will become open ended and risk not addressing what is important to the evaluators. The better we understand the requirement, the more likely we are to create a winning technical solution.

Step 2 – Create candidate technical solutions

Next, let's look at various technical solutions or approaches to doing the work. We like to have more than one approach since we want to trade off the merits of each as we close in on our preferred solution. The chosen solution should be technically sound, complete, logical, and internally consistent. In other words, we need an excellent technical solution that achieves what the customer has asked for, addresses the appropriate requirements in the RFP, and has no weaknesses in its approach.

Keep the alternative solutions handy since we may want to discuss them in our proposal as alternatives we considered when developing our technical solution, but discarded because our chosen approach is superior. This tradeoff discussion can be an effective way of ghosting another bidder's approach, especially if they have chosen to propose one of the alternative approaches that we discarded.

10 steps to creating high-scoring proposals
A modern perspective on proposal development and what really matters

Step 3 – Engineer in your proposal evaluation strengths

When the government evaluates your technical approach, they will be looking for proposal strengths. These are the features of your solution that either 1) increase the likelihood of successful contract accomplishment or 2) exceed a contract requirement in a way that is beneficial to the government. There may be other features that are evaluated as proposal strengths depending on the mission of the agency, for example, lethality of the system, safety inherent in your solution, etc.

Make sure you agree on how the government is going to define proposal strengths. In our experience, the definition is pretty narrow and may cause a lot of the features of your solution to be noted as interesting, but not scored as proposal strengths.

As a solution development team, we must comb through your technical solution and identify all features that might be scored as strengths since these will need to be highlighted in your proposal. If we don't find evaluation strengths in your solution, then we go back and rework the solution until we have engineered features into the solution that can be scored as proposals strengths. The more strengths, the better the proposal will score.

For each proposed evaluation strength, make sure you include evidence to support your claims, and clearly delineate the benefit of each feature to ensure that the

10 steps to creating high-scoring proposals
A modern perspective on proposal development and what really matters

benefit tracks with the definition of what proposal strengths are for your solution.

Step 4 – Bring in the innovation

There is a natural tension between the need to propose proven solutions and the need to continually improve the way you propose to perform the work being bid. If you are justifying your solution by saying, "This is the way we always do this work," or "This is how we did it last time," then challenge your engineers to do it better, quicker, and cheaper.

Build innovation into your solution and show the government that you are indeed committed to improving the way work is done—and offer real solutions to do this. Make creativity part of your solutioning process, and always remember that last year's breakthrough in technology can become this year's obsolete solution.

Step 5 – Reduce the cost

Challenge your technical team to engineer cost avoidance and cost reduction into their solutions. If it cost you a certain amount to do this work last time, then figure out how you can do it for less. Be mindful that you need to engineer cost reductions into your solution or technical approach when you are creating it, not wait for executive management to force it into your proposal in the final days of the pricing exercise.

10 steps to creating high-scoring proposals
A modern perspective on proposal development and what really matters

Make these 5 steps part of your solutioning process, and you will consistently produce technical solutions that score well—hopefully bringing you more victories!

From WashingtonTechnology.com.

Made in the USA
Middletown, DE
06 August 2018